Fresh and Flavorful Salad Recipes

From Simple Greens to Creative Combinations, Discover the Joy of Healthy Eating

Sophia Taylor

Copyright © 2023 - All rights reserved.

The content contained within this book may not be reproduced, duplicated, or transmitted without direct written permission from the author or the publisher.

Under no circumstances will any blame or legal responsibility be held against the publisher, or author, for any damages, reparation, or monetaryloss due to the information contained within this book. Either directly or indirectly.

Legal Notice:

This book is copyright protected. This book is only for personal use. You cannot amend, distribute, sell, use, quote, or paraphrase any part, or the content within this book, without the consent of the author or publisher.

Disclaimer Notice:

Please note the information contained within this document is for educational and entertainment purposes only. All effort has been executed to present accurate, up-to-date, and reliable, complete information. No warranties of any kind are declared or implied. Readers acknowledge that the author is not engaging in the rendering of legal, financial, medical, or professional advice. The content within this book has been derived from various sources. Please consult a licensed professional before attempting any techniques outlined in this book.

By reading this document, the reader agrees that under no circumstances is the author responsible for any losses, direct or indirect, which are incurred as a result of the use of the information contained within this document, including, but not limited to, — errors, omissions, or inaccuracies.

TABLE OF CONTENT

INTRODUCTION

Salads are an incredibly versatile meal option that can be customized to fit any taste preference or dietary need. They are perfect for those who are health-conscious and looking to incorporate more fresh fruits and vegetables into their diet, as well as for those who are looking for a satisfying and filling meal option.

The Salad Freak Cookbook offers a wide range of recipes that are not only delicious but also packed with essential nutrients that are necessary for maintaining good health. Each recipe is designed to be colorful and flavorful, making them a feast for the eyes and taste buds.

One of the great things about salads is that they can be easily adapted to fit a variety of dietary needs. The Salad Freak Cookbook features a range of vegetarian and vegan recipes that are perfect for those who are looking to cut back on their meat consumption or follow a plant-based diet. Additionally, many of the recipes can be easily modified to accommodate specific dietary needs or restrictions, such as gluten-free or dairy-free diets.

This cookbook is great for both beginners and seasoned chefs because of the variety of salad recipes and helpful instructions it provides. In addition to providing a diverse selection of salad recipes, the Salad Freak Cookbook also offers valuable tips and tricks for creating the perfect salad. You'll learn how to properly wash and store your produce, how to create flavorful dressings and toppings, and how to mix and match ingredients to create endless flavor combinations.

Overall, the Salad Freak Cookbook is a complete guide to making tasty, healthy salads that are great for any meal or event. Anyone who values eating healthy, delicious food that is also visually appealing and full of flavor will find a wealth of inspiration in this cookbook. It has a lot of recipes and helpful tips and tricks. So, if you love salads or just want to eat more plant-based meals, the Salad Freak Cookbook is the perfect resource for you.

POTATO SALAD

GERMAN POTATO SALAD

Prep Time: 20 Minutes

Cook Time: 30 Minutes

Total Time: 50 Minutes

Serve: 6

Ingredients

- 2 pounds waxy potatoes
- 6-8 slices bacon, finely diced
- ½ cup of finely chopped onion
- ¾ cup of beef stock and 6 tbsp white vinegar
- 1 tsp mustard, Dijon or mild German mustard
- 2 tbsp vegetable oil, preferably sunflower or avocado oil
- 1 tsp sugar
- ½ tsp salt, or more to taste
- ¼ tsp black pepper, freshly ground
- 1 tbsp chopped parsley or chives

Instructions

1. First, boil the potatoes in a large pot with an inch of water and high heat until soft, which should take about 20 minutes, depending on how big the potatoes are.

2. In the meantime, make the dressing. In a pan over medium heat, cook the bacon until it is crispy. Next, take the bacon out of the pan and set it aside. Leave the fat in the pan. Now, add the onion to the pan and cook it for about 3–4 minutes, until it is clear but not brown. Get the beef broth boiling. Lastly, turn the heat down to low and add the vinegar, mustard, oil, sugar, salt, and pepper.

3. Let the potatoes cool down a bit so that you can handle them. They need to be peeled. Cut the potatoes into 1/4-inch slices or cubes and put them in a large bowl.

4. Pour the hot sauce on top of the potatoes. After you mix the salad, gently fold in the bacon pieces. Let the salad sit out at room temperature for at least 20 minutes before serving so the potatoes can soak up the flavor of the dressing.

RED POTATO SALAD

Prep Time: 15 Minutes

Cook Time: 20 Minutes

Chill Time: 60 Minutes

Total Time: 1 Hour 35 Minutes

Serve: 6

Ingredients

- 2/3 c. mayonnaise
- 1/2 c. sour cream
- 2 tbsp. white wine vinegar
- 1 tbsp. Dijon mustard
- 1 tsp. kosher salt
- 1 tsp. ground black pepper
- 2 stalks of celery, chopped
- 1/4 c. chopped dill

- 6 slices cooked bacon, chopped

Instructions

1. First, put the potatoes in a big pot and cover them with water. Add salt to taste. Now, bring the water to a boil on high heat, then lower the heat to medium and let it simmer. Now, cook for about 20 minutes, or until you can stick a fork into the potatoes. Drain the potatoes, wait a few minutes for them to cool down, and then cut them in half or four. (depending on the size of the potatoes).
2. Give it about an hour to cool down.
3. In a large mixing bowl, mix the mayonnaise, sour cream, vinegar, mustard, salt, and pepper with a whisk.
4. Put the potatoes, celery, and dill in the bowl with the dressing. Stir slowly to blend. Just before serving, put some crispy bacon on top.

SOUTHERN POTATO SALAD

Prep Time: 20 Minutes

Cook Time: 15 Minutes

Total Time: 35 Minutes

Serve: 8

Ingredients

- 3 pounds peeled and cubed Russet, Yukon gold, or red potatoes

- 1 cup of mayonnaise
- 1 tbsp yellow mustard
- ¼ cup of chopped sweet pickles or sweet relish
- 2 tsp. granulated sugar
- 2 tsp apple cider vinegar
- ½ tsp garlic powder
- 5 shelled and diced hard-boiled eggs
- 4 finely diced green onions
- 2 finely diced celery stalks Black pepper, to taste kosher salt

Instructions

1. Cover the potatoes with cold water in a large pot. Place over high heat and cook just until the food is soft enough to cut with a fork. Watch the potatoes carefully because if they cook too long, they will get mushy.
2. When the potatoes are soft, drain them in a strainer and let them cool while you make the other salad ingredients.
3. Now, add mayonnaise, yellow mustard, chopped pickles, sugar, apple cider vinegar, and garlic powder to a large bowl and mix well. Whisk together.
4. Add the diced hard-boiled eggs, green onions, and celery to the bowl with the potatoes. Stir slowly to blend.
5. Taste and add as much kosher salt and black pepper as you like.

SWEET POTATO SALAD

Prep Time: 5 Minutes

Cook Time: 350 Minutes

Total Time: 40 Minutes

Serve: 6

Ingredients

- 1 red bell pepper, diced
- 2 tbsp lime juice
- 1 cup of corn from a can or cooked, if you want
- 1/2 tsp salt, and pepper if you want it
- 3/4 cup of chopped fresh cilantro
- 4 peeled and chopped medium sweet potatoes (2 lb before peeling)
- 1 can of black beans, or 1 1/2 cups of cooked beans
- 2 tsp of chopped garlic
- 3 tsp of oil or spray (for fat-free option)
- 1 diced onion

Instructions

1. Combine the sweet potatoes and onions with 1 1/2 tbsp of oil (or cooking spray) and the garlic. Now, sprinkle with salt and pepper to taste, and arrange in a single layer on two baking sheets lined with parchment paper.
2. Place on the middle rack of a cold oven, then heat to 450 F. Bake the potatoes for 35 minutes, or until soft.
3. Mix the sweet potatoes with the rest of the ingredients in a large bowl.

4. Serve either hot or cold.

VEGAN POTATO SALAD

Prep Time: 10 Minutes

Cook Time: 15 Minutes

Total Time: 25 Minutes

Serve: 4

Ingredients

- 600g baby new potatoes, cut in half; those are bigger
- 2 tsp of white wine vinegar
- 2 tsp of extra virgin olive oil
- 120g vegan mayonnaise
- 1½ tsp Dijon mustard
- 1 shallot, or half of a red onion, chopped finely
- 2 tsp of chopped capers, if large
- A small handful of chopped parsley
- A small handful of chopped chives.

Instructions

1 Salt the potatoes and cover them with cold water in a pan. Now, bring to a boil and let simmer for 15–20 minutes, or until the vegetables gets a little soft. Drain and leave in a colander for 5 minutes to steam-dry. If the skin is papery and coming off, you can rub it off if you want to.

2   Put the potatoes in a bowl and add the vinegar, olive oil, and seasonings. Toss well, then set aside to cool.

3   Mix in the herbs, mayonnaise, mustard, shallot, capers, and capers. (saving a little to garnish). Check the seasoning and, if you like, add a little more salt or vinegar. Sprinkle the rest of the herbs on top and serve.

CAULIFLOWER POTATO SALAD

Prep Time: 15 Minutes

Cook Time: 20 Minutes

Total Time: 35 Minutes

Serve: 6

Ingredients

- 1 head of cauliflower cut into pieces that are 1/2 inch long
- 1 tbsp olive oil
- To taste, add salt and pepper

Dressing

- ¼ cup of avocado mayonnaise
- 2 tbsp Dijon mustard
- 2 tbsp dill pickle juice
- ¼ cup of finely chopped celery
- ¼ cup of finely chopped red onions
- ¼ cup of finely chopped dill pickles
- 2 hard-boiled eggs, diced

- Dash paprika
- Dill for garnishing

Instructions

1. Preheat the oven to 400°F and put parchment paper on a baking sheet. Salt, pepper, and olive oil the cauliflower, and spread it out evenly on a baking sheet that has been prepared. Bake for 15–20 minutes in an oven that has already been heated until the cauliflower is soft enough to cut with a fork. Set aside so it can cool.
2. Mix the dressing by whisking the mayonnaise, mustard, and dill pickle juice in a large bowl. Add the chopped celery, red onions, pickles, cauliflower, eggs, and season with salt and pepper. Mix gently to make sure everything is evenly distributed.
3. Garnish with chives and paprika.

DEVILED EGG POTATO SALAD

Prep Time: 30 Minutes

Cook Time: 15 Minutes

Total Time: 45 Minutes

Serve: 12

Ingredients

- 4 pounds potatoes about 8 large
- 12 hard boiled eggs
- ½ cups of mayo
- ¼ cup of mustard
- 1 tbsp white vinegar
- 2 tbsp dill relish
- Salt & pepper to taste

Instructions

1   Cut the potatoes in half. Boil potatoes in a large pot with enough water to cover until tender, about 15 minutes. When finished, drain and place in a bowl to chill in the refrigerator. Peel the potatoes with a paring knife when they are cools down enough to handle but still warm. After that, dice the potatoes.
2   Hard boiled eggs should be peeled and cut in half. Set aside the egg whites and combine the yolks in a mixing bowl.
3   Next, mash the egg yolks as you would for deviled eggs.
4   Whisk together the mayonnaise, mustard, and vinegar with the mashed egg yolks until smooth and creamy.
5   Fold the dill relish into the egg yolk mixture.

6   Chop the egg whites and combine them with the diced potatoes. To combine, toss gently.Season with salt and pepper to taste.

7   Chill for at least 1 hour, preferably overnight, before serving.

LOADED BAKED POTATO SALAD

Prep Time: 20 Minutes

Cook Time: 60 Minutes

Chill Time: 3 Hours

Total Time: 4 hours 20 minutes

Serve: 12

Ingredients

- 4 pounds of russet potatoes
- 1-2 tbsp of olive oil
- 3 tbsp apple cider vinegar
- 1 cup of mayonnaise 6 chopped green onions
- ¾ cup of soured cream or Greek yogurt
- 1 tsp kosher salt
- 1 tsp of freshly ground black pepper
- 12 ounces of bacon that has been cooked, let cool, and then chopped
- 1 ½ cups of shredded medium cheddar cheese

Instructions

1   Set the oven temperature to 400° F.

2   Put the clean potatoes on a baking sheet and poke them 4 to 5 times with a fork. Coat lightly with olive oil, sprinkle with kosher salt, and bake for 50 to 60 minutes, or until a cake tester or skewer can go through it easily.

3   Next, take the food out of the oven and give it 5 minutes to cool down. When the potatoes are cool enough to touch, peel them and cut them into small pieces, throwing away the skins. It's fine if the potato flesh breaks up and gets shaggy; put it all in a large mixing bowl. Sprinkle the hot potatoes with the apple cider vinegar and let them sit for 15–30 minutes, or until they are cool.

4   Meantime, cook the bacon in a big pan or the oven, drain it, and set it aside to cool. Crumble into bite-size pieces.

5   In a small bowl, mix the mayo and sour cream together. Season the food with the kosher salt and pepper.

6   When the potatoes are cool, pour the mayonnaise mixture over them and add the crumbled bacon, green onion, and cheddar cheese. Mix the ingredients together gently. Add more salt and pepper to your taste. Before serving, put in the fridge for 3 hours or up to a full day. You can keep this in the fridge for up to 4 days.

MUSTARD POTATO SALAD

Prep Time: 15 Minutes

Cook Time: 10 Minutes

Total Time: 25 Minutes

Serve: 8

Ingredients

- 3 tbsp yellow mustard
- 1/2 cup of pickle relish plus 2 tbsp juice, dill or sweet
- 1/4 tsp salt
- 2 celery ribs, finely diced
- 1 tbsp salt
- 3 pounds russet potatoes, peeled and cubed
- 1/4 to 1/2 tsp black pepper
- 1/2 medium sweet onion, diced
- 4 large hard-boiled eggs, peeled and chopped
- 1/4 tsp paprika
- 3/4 cup of mayonnaise

Instructions

1. Put potatoes in a medium pot and add enough water to cover them. Get it to boil. Add salt and turn down the heat to keep a simmer going. Simmer for 10 to 12 minutes or until a fork can easily go through the vegetables.
2. Well, drain the potatoes and put them back in the hot pot. This will make the water dry up.

3 Put the celery, onion, eggs, relish, and juice from the pickles in a large bowl.

4 Add potatoes, mustard, mayonnaise, salt and pepper.

5 Stir well, and as you stir, cut up some of the potatoes.

6 Now, put it in the fridge for at least two hours.

7 Sprinkle with paprika just before serving.

EGG POTATO SALAD

Prep Time: 20 Minutes

Cook Time: 30 Minutes

Refrigerate Time: 60 Minutes

Total Time: 1 Hour 50 Minutes

Serve: 6

Ingredients

- ½ cup of Mayonnaise
- 1 tsp Salt plus 1 tbsp to cook the potatoes
- 1 tbsp Dijon Mustard
- 2 pounds of Gold Potatoes
- ¼ tsp Black Pepper
- 2 tbsp Apple Cider Vinegar
- Eggs hard-boiled, peeled and cut into bite-sized pieces
- 2 tbsp Green Onions chopped (plus a little extra for garnish, optional)
- 1 Celery Rib finely diced

- ½ tsp Celery Seed

Instructions

Make the dressing

1. Add the mayonnaise, apple cider vinegar, Dijon mustard, celery seed, salt, and pepper to
   a jar or bowl. Stir vigorously with a fork or small whisk until the ingredients are combined and the dressing is creamy. Refrigerate until ready to use.

Cook the potatoes

1. Put the potatoes in a big pot and pour enough water over them to cover them by about 2 inches. Put the pot on high heat and bring the water to a full boil, which will take about 8 to 10 minutes.
2. When the water is boiling vigorously, add 1 tbsp of salt.
3. Boil the potatoes for 20-30 minutes or until they are fork-tender. A small, sharp knife or fork should slide in and out without resistance.
4. Use a large strainer to drain them and let them cool.
5. Boil the eggs while the potatoes cook:
6. Carefully place the eggs in a medium saucepan and cover them completely with water. Place the pan over high heat and bring the water to a full boil. Once the water is boiling vigorously, turn off the heat, cover the pan and let the eggs sit for 10 minutes. Drain the water and rinse the eggs with cold water. Lastly, peel them when they are cool enough to handle.

Build the potato salad

1. Cut the potato into 1½ – 2 inch pieces, make them bite-sized. Remove and discard the peel from the potatoes; they should come right off. If some pieces stay behind that's ok because the peel is super thin.
2. Place them in a large bowl.
3. Cut the eggs into bite-sized pieces and add them to the bowl with the potatoes.
4. Sprinkle in the celery and green onions and pour the dressing.
5. Use a spatula to gently stir and toss until the ingredients are combined and everything is coated with the dressing.
6. Cover the bowl and refrigerate until it is chilled. Stir well and garnish with extra sliced onions before serving.

Instructions

Potatoes Should Be Cooked

1. Cover the potatoes with 1 1/2 inches of water in a large pot. Season with salt to taste, one tsp per quart of water.
2. Cook for around 15 to 20 minutes, or until easily pierced with a fork. Now, bring the water to a boil, then reduce to a simmer (boiling the potatoes can cause them to collide and break apart).
3. Prepare an ice bath in the meantime. Half-fill a medium bowl with ice and half-full with cold water. Place the potatoes in an ice bath to cool. Peel the potatoes after they have cooled by gently pinching the skin and pulling it away.
4 Now, place the peeled potatoes in a large mixing bowl and chop them into bite-size chunks. Sprinkle the vinegar over the potatoes and season with salt to taste.

Onions "De-flame"

5   Put the onions in a small bowl and cover with cold water while the potatoes cook. After 10 minutes, rinse thoroughly. This step helps to reduce the raw onion flavor.

Make A Salad With Potatoes

6   Combine the sour cream, mayonnaise, and mustard in a mixing bowl.

7   Combine the sour cream mixture, de-flamed onions, celery, pickles, eggs, and herbs with the potatoes. Gently combine, taking care not to over-mash the potatoes.

8   Season to taste with salt and pepper. If you have the time, chill for at least 30 minutes before serving.

GREEN SALAD

CUCUMBER SALAD

Prep Time: 10 Minutes

Chill Time: 3 Hours

Total Time: 3 Hours 10 Minutes

Serve: 6

Ingredients

- 2 small cucumbers, sliced thinly
- 1/3 cup of apple juice or white vinegar
- 1/3 cup of of water
- 2 tsp of sugar
- 1/2 tsp salt
- 1/8 tsp pepper

If you want, chopped fresh dill weed or parsley

Instructions

1. Put cukes in a small bowl made of glass or plastic.
2. Shake everything else, except the dill weed, in a container with a tight lid. Put on top of cucumbers.
3. Now, cover and chill for at least 3 hours to let the flavors come together.
4. Drain cucumbers. Sprinkle with dill weed. Store covered in refrigerator.

ESCAROLE SALAD WITH RED QUINOA AND HAZELNUTS

Prep Time: 20 Minutes

Chill Time: 20 Minutes

Total Time: 40 Minutes

Serve: 6

Ingredients

- 1/4 cup of red quinoa, rinsed and drained
- 1/4 cup of plus 2 tbsp of extra-virgin olive oil
- 3 tbsp apple cider vinegar
- 1 tbsp plus 1 tsp honey
- Fine sea salt
- Pepper
- 1 head of escarole, chopped into bite-size pieces
- 1 Granny Smith apple—halved, cored and thinly sliced on a mandoline 1/2 cup of toasted hazelnuts, chopped

Instructions

1. First, in a medium saucepan of boiling water, cook the quinoa just until tender, about 10 minutes. Drain well and spread out on a baking sheet to cool.
2. Now in a large bowl, whisk the olive oil with the vinegar and honey. Season with salt and pepper. Add the escarole, apple, hazelnuts and quinoa and toss to coat. Season with salt and pepper and serve.

CHARRED CABBAGE SALAD WITH PECAN DUKKAH AND CHILE-LIME BUTTER

Prep Time: 15 Minutes | Cook Time: 15 Minutes | Chill Time: 15 Minutes

Total Time: 45 Minutes | Serve: 6

Ingredients

Pecan Dukkah

- ½ cup of pecan halves
- ¼ cup of white sesame seeds
- 1 ½ tsp coriander seeds
- ¾ tsp cumin seeds
- 1 tsp kosher salt
- ½ tsp Aleppo pepper

Chile-Lime Butter

- 5 medium (1/10 ounce total) de árbol chiles, toasted
- ¼ tsp cumin seeds, toasted
- 1 cup of unsalted butter, softened
- 2 tsp grated lime zest plus 1 1/2 Tbsp fresh juice (from 1 lime)
- 2 tsp kosher salt
- 1 medium garlic clove, grated (1/4 tsp.)
- ¼ tsp smoked paprika
- ¼ tsp black pepper

Charred Cabbage Salad

- 2 tbsp Chile-Lime Butter, softened
- 1 tbsp fresh lime juice
- 1 small (2 pound) savoy cabbage, halved lengthwise, cored, and leaves separated

- 3 tbsp olive oil

- ½ tsp kosher salt, plus more to taste

- ¼ tsp black pepper, plus more to taste

- 1 tbsp Pecan Dukkah

- 2 tbsp roughly chopped mixed fresh herbs (such as dill, chives, mint, cilantro, andchervil)

Instructions

Prepare the Pecan Dukkah

1   Get the oven ready at 325°F. On a baking sheet with a rim, spread out the pecans, sesame seeds, coriander seeds, and cumin seeds.

2   Bake in an oven that has already been heated for 9 to 10 minutes, until lightly browned and fragrant. Give it about 15 minutes to cool down completely.

3   Put the mixture in a food processor and pulse it 8 to 10 times until the pecans are finely chopped.

4   Move the mixture to a small bowl and add the salt and Aleppo. Now, store at room temperature for up to 3 weeks in a container that keeps out air.

Get the Chile-Lime Butter ready

1   Put the chiles and cumin seeds in a spice grinder and run it for about 30 seconds, or until the mixture looks like a fine powder. Put butter, lime zest and juice, salt, garlic, smoked paprika, and black pepper in the large bowl of a stand mixer that comes with a whisk attachment. Beat the mixture for 1 minute to 1 minute and 30 seconds on medium-high speed, or until the butter is light and creamy. Move to a container that won't let air in and store in the fridge for up to two weeks.

Make the Salad of Charred Cabbage

2   Set aside the Chile-Lime Butter and lime juice in a large bowl. Get the grill hot (450°F to 500°F) on high.

3   In a separate large bowl, mix cabbage leaves, oil, salt, and black pepper until the leaves are evenly coated. If you need to, put the leaves on oiled grill grates in batches. Grill, uncovered, and flip the leaves often for 2 to 5 minutes, until some spots are blackened. Don't let the leaves catch fire; turn them over often and move them around the grill as needed.

4   Add the charred leaves to the Chile-Lime Butter mixture in a large bowl and gently toss until the butter has melted and the leaves are evenly coated, about 1 minute.

5   Depending on your taste, add more salt and black pepper. Place the leaves on a large plate and sprinkle them with Pecan Dukkah and fresh herbs. Warm is best.

LITTLE GEM SALAD WITH LEMON VINAIGRETTE

Prep Time: 18 Minutes

Cook Time: 12 Minutes

Total Time: 30 Minutes

Serve: 4

Ingredients

- 1 cup of halves of walnuts
- 1 tbsp oil from walnuts
- Kosher salt
- 1 small chopped shallot
- 1/4 cup of fresh lemon juice
- 1 tbsp Champagne vinegar
- 1/2 cup of extra-virgin olive oil
- Pepper, freshly grounded
- 4 ounces of sliced yellow squash
- 3 thin slices of red onion, cut into rings
- 4 heads of Little Gem lettuce
- 1/4 cup of of freshly grated Pecorino Romano cheese, plus more for serving

Instructions

1. Turn the oven on to 350°. Toast the walnuts on a pie plate for 12 minutes, until they are golden brown. Let the nuts cool, then cut them into large pieces.

2   Move to a bowl and toss with a pinch of salt and the walnut oil. Mix the shallot, lemon juice, and vinegar in a small bowl. Add salt to taste. Let stand for 10 minutes. Add the olive oil slowly and season with pepper.

3   Mix the squash, onion, lettuce, walnuts, pecorino, and half of the dressing in a large bowl and serve. Save the rest of the dressing for later.

LEMONY WALDORF SALAD

Prep Time: 17 Minutes

Cook Time: 8 Minutes

Total Time: 25 Minutes

Serve: 6

Ingredients

- ½ cup of walnut halves (2 ounces)
- 1 tbsp minced shallot
- ½ tsp finely grated lemon zest
- 2 tbsp fresh lemon juice
- 1 tbsp white wine vinegar
- ¼ cup of plus 2 tbsp canola oil
- 2 ¼ tbsp walnut oil
- ½ tsp ground cumin
- Salt and freshly ground pepper
- 2 cups of shredded romaine lettuce (4 ounces)
- 4 large radishes (halved lengthwise and thinly sliced crosswise (1 cup))

- 1 ¼ cups of chopped celery leaves (from 4 inner ribs plus 1/4 cup of chopped celery leaves)
- 1 small head of frisée (6 ounces coarsely chopped)
- ¼ cup of golden raisins
- 1 Fuji apple (peeled, quartered, cored and thinly sliced crosswise)

Instructions

1. Turn the oven on to 350°. Spread the walnuts out in a pie plate and toast them for about 8 minutes, or until they are golden brown and smell good. Let the nuts cool down, and then break them up.
2. Meanwhile, in a large bowl, combine the shallot and lemon zest with the lemon juice and vinegar. Whisk in the canola and walnut oils and the cumin. Season the dressing with salt and pepper.
3. Add the shredded romaine lettuce to the bowl along with the toasted walnuts, radishes, sliced celery hearts, celery leaves, chopped frisée, raisins and apple. Toss well and serve right away.

GREENS, AVOCADO, AND BLUEBERRY SALAD

Prep Time: 20 Minutes

Cook Time: 0 Minutes

Total Time: 20 Minutes

Serve: 6

Ingredients

- Sesame-Honey-Ginger Dressing:
- ¼ cup of sesame oil (untoasted)
- ¼ cup of white balsamic vinegar with honey and ginger (such as LeRoux)
- 1 tsp herbes de Provence
- ¾ tsp blueberry-honey sea salt, like Martha's Vineyard Sea Salt., and more to suit

Salad

- 1 (roughly 3 1/2 ounces) Head of Boston lettuce, leaves pulled apart (about 4 cups)
- 4 cups of arugula that is loosely packed (about 3 ounces)
- 2 cups of of mizuna, not tightly packed (about 2 ounces)
- 1 small red onion, thinly sliced (about 6 ounces), (about 1 cup)
- 1 medium avocado, about 6 ounces, cut into 1/2-inch pieces (about 3/4 cup of). ¾ cup of fresh blueberries (about 4 ounces)

Instructions

1 To make the honey-sesame-ginger dressing:
2 First in a medium bowl, whisk together the oil, vinegar, herbes de Provence, and salt until the salt is gone. Add more salt to suit your taste.

Preparing the salad

3 In a large bowl, mix together the lettuce, arugula, mizuna, onion, avocado, and blueberries.
4 Pour 1/3 cup of dressing over the salad and toss to coat. Add more dressing if you want.

GRILLED ASPARAGUS SALAD

Prep Time: 15 Minutes

Cook Time: 5 Minutes

Chill Time: 20 Minutes

Total Time: 40 Minutes

Serve: 6

Ingredients

- 1 pound asparagus
- 1/2 cup of extra-virgin olive oil, plus more for brushing
- Freshly ground pepper and Salt
- 4 lightly packed cups of of mesclun
- 1 seedless cucumber, cut into 1/2-inch dice
- 1 cup of grape tomatoes, halved
- 1 cup of drained and rinsed canned chickpeas
- 1/2 cup of pitted kalamata olives, coarsely chopped (3 ounces)
- 8 ounces sharp white cheddar, cut into 1/4-inch dice
- 3 tbsp fresh orange juice
- 1 tbsp fresh lemon juice
- 1 tbsp red wine vinegar
- 1 tsp Dijon mustard
- 1 tsp grainy mustard
- 1 tbsp chopped tarragon
- 3 cups of pita chips

Instructions

1   Start a grill or preheat a grill pan. Salt and pepper the asparagus after rubbing it with oil. Grill over high heat, turning often, for

about 5 minutes, or until tender. Let the asparagus cool, then cut it into 1-inch pieces.

2   In a large bowl, combine the mesclun with the grilled asparagus, cucumber, tomatoes, chickpeas, olives, and cheese.

3   In a bowl, combine the orange juice, lemon juice, vinegar, both mustards, and a pinch of salt and pepper. Gradually whisk in the 1/2 cup of oil until the mixture is smooth, then add the tarragon. Lastly, pour the dressing over the salad and mix it together. Pita chips can be used as a garnish.

SPINACH AND SMOKED SALMON SALAD WITH LEMON-DILL DRESSING

Prep Time: 15 Minutes

Cook Time: 0 Minutes

Total Time: 15 Minutes

Serve: 4

Ingredients

- 3 tbsp extra-virgin olive oil
- 2 tbsp fresh lemon juice
- 2 tbsp of dill, chopped
- Kosher salt and pepper that was just ground
- 8 cups of of Baby spinach (7 ounces)
- 6 ounces of smoked salmon that has been sliced thinly and cut into 1/2-inch ribbons
- 1 medium English cucumber, peeled, cut in half lengthwise, seeded, and sliced very thinly4 radishes, cut in half and sliced thin

- 2 thin slices of scallions

Instructions

- Mix the olive oil, lemon juice, and dill together in a large bowl. Add salt and pepper to taste.
- Now, add the spinach, smoked salmon, cucumber, radishes, and scallions to the bowl and mix well.
- Serve the salad by putting it on plates.

CHOPPED ITALIAN SALAD

Prep Time: 15 Minutes

Cook Time: 0 Minutes

Total Time: 15 Minutes

Serve: 4

Ingredients

- 1 head romaine lettuce (about 1 1/4 pounds), cut into 1-inch squares (about 3 quarts)
- 1/4 pound sliced pepperoni, chopped
- 1/3 cup of drained sliced pimientos (one 4-ounce jar)
- 1/3 cup of chopped red onion
- 1 1/2 cups of drained, rinsed, and chopped canned artichoke hearts (one 15-ounce can), or
- 1 1/2 cups of pitted and chopped green or black olives

- 3 tbsp red- or white-wine vinegar
- 1/4 cup of olive oil
- 1/2 tsp salt
- 1/4 tsp fresh-ground black pepper
- 1/2 cup of grated Parmesan

Instructions

1. In a large glass or stainless-steel bowl, combine the romaine, pepperoni, pimientos, onion, and the artichoke hearts or olives. Toss to combine.
2. Add the vinegar, oil, salt, pepper, and Parmesan to the bowl.
3. Toss thoroughly to combine the ingredients.

ARUGULA SALAD WITH OLIVES, FETA, AND DILL

Prep Time: 20 Minutes

Cook Time: 0 Minutes

Chill Time: 60 Minutes

Total Time: 1 Hour 20 Minutes

Serve: 10

Ingredients

- 1 red onion (very thinly sliced)
- 1 garlic clove (minced)
- 1 cup of pitted kalamata olives (coarsely chopped)

- ½ cup of plus 2 tbsp extra-virgin olive oil
- ¼ cup of plus 2 tbsp red wine vinegar
- Salt and freshly ground pepper
- 3 tbsp chopped fresh dill
- 1 cup of crumbled Greek feta cheese (5 ounces)
- 14 ounces baby arugula (20 cups)

Instructions

1. In a large bowl, mix the oil, vinegar, salt, and pepper with the onion, garlic, and olives.
2. Let sit for 1 hour at room temperature.
3. Mix in the dill and feta, then gently toss in the arugula.
4. Serve at once.

CHOPPED SALAD WITH BLUE CHEESE DRESSING

Prep Time: 15 Minutes

Cook Time: 10 Minutes

Total Time: 25 Minutes

Serve: 6

Ingredients

- 1/2 cup of walnuts
- 1 tbsp of shallots that have been chopped very finely
- 1 tbsp of shallot that has been chopped very finely

- 1 1/2 tsp of Dijon mustard
- 3 tbsp of sherry vinegar
- Kosher salt and black pepper, ground
- 1/4 cup of extra-virgin olive oil
- 4 ounces of crumbled blue cheese
- 2 romaine hearts, cut in half lengthwise and sliced thinly across the middle.
- 1/2 bulb of fennel, cored and chopped finely
- 2 carrots, chopped finely
- 1/2 cucumber without seeds, seeded and cut into 1/2-inch dice
- 1 Fuji apple, cut into 1/2-inch dice
- 1 Hass avocado, cut into 1/2-inch dice
- 2 tbsp of thinly shredded basil leaves

Instructions

1. Turn the oven on to 350°. Spread the walnuts out in a pie plate and toast them until they are golden, about 10 minutes. Let it cool, then chop it up roughly.
2. Whisk the shallot, Dijon mustard, and sherry vinegar together in a large bowl. Add a lot of salt and pepper. Whisk until smooth, then add the olive oil.
3. Whisk in half of the blue cheese until the dressing is smooth and creamy.
4. Salt and pepper the lettuce, fennel, carrots, cucumber, apple, avocado, basil, and walnuts. Mix the salad with the dressing well.
5. Add the rest of the blue cheese on top, and serve right away.

BOSTON LETTUCE WITH CILANTRO AND WALNUTS

Prep Time: 10 Minutes

Cook Time: 0 Minutes

Total Time: 10 Minutes

Serve: 8

Ingredients

- 2 tbsp vegetable oil
- 2 tbsp white wine vinegar
- 1 tbsp freshly squeezed lemon juice
- Salt and freshly ground black pepper
- 10 medium radishes, very thinly sliced on a mandoline
- 5 scallions, thinly sliced
- 1 head Boston lettuce, small leaves left whole and large leaves torn
- 2 tbsp chopped cilantro leaves
- 3 tbsp chopped walnuts

Instructions

1. In a large bowl, whisk the oil with the vinegar and lemon juice and season with salt and pepper.
2. Add the radishes, scallions, lettuce and cilantro and toss well.
3. Garnish with the walnuts and serve right away.

SEAWEED AND GREENS SALAD

Prep Time: 20 Minutes

Cook Time: 0 Minutes

Total Time: 20 Minutes

Serve: 4

Ingredients

- 1 tbsp finely chopped shallot
- 1 tbsp fresh lemon juice
- 1 tsp Dijon mustard and ¼ tsp honey
- 2 tbsp neutral cooking oil (such as grapeseed)
- 1 tbsp extra-virgin olive oil
- ⅛ tsp black pepper, plus more to taste
- .50 tsp fine sea salt; add more to taste

Salt

- 8 cups of leafy salad greens, torn into bite-size pieces
- 1 cup of frozen ready-cut kelp
- .50 cups of radishes cut into thin slices
- .50 cups of cucumber cut in diagonal slices 1/8 inch thick
- .50 cups of dried dulse leaves, whole (such as Maine Coast Sea Vegetables)
- ¾ cup of diagonally sliced (1/8-inch-thick) carrots
- .50 cup of dried whole-leaf Irish moss, like bite-sized Maine Coast Sea Vegetables Black pepper, to taste and Kosher salt, to taste

Instructions

1   To make the dressing:

2   In a small bowl, mix the vinegar, shallot, lemon juice, mustard, and honey until they are all mixed together. Next, add the oils in a thin, steady stream and whisk until the mixture is smooth. Whisk in salt and pepper.

To make the salad

1. Put salad greens, kelp, carrots, radishes, cucumber, dulse, and Irish moss in a large bowl and mix them all together. Lastly, pour the dressing over the salad and gently toss to coat. Add more salt and pepper to taste to the salad. Serve right away.

CELERY, GRILLED GRAPE, AND MUSHROOM SALAD

Prep Time: 15 Minutes

Cook Time: 10 Minutes

Chill Time: 20 Minutes

Total Time: 45 Minutes

Serve: 6

Ingredients

- 2 tbsp white wine vinegar
- 2 tsp fresh lemon juice
- 1/2 tsp celery seeds
- 1/4 tsp Dijon mustard
- 2 small garlic cloves, minced

- 1/2 cup of plus 1 tbsp extra-virgin olive oil, plus more for brushing
- 1/4 cup of roasted almond oil
- Salt and freshly ground pepper
- 1/2 cup of flat-leaf parsley leaves
- 1/2 cup of tender celery leaves (from one head)
- 1/4 cup of salted roasted almonds, chopped
- 1 pound king oyster mushrooms, sliced lengthwise 1/4 inch thick
- 2 cups of green grapes (12 ounces)
- 2 heads butter lettuce, leaves separated
- 2 cups of very thinly sliced celery

Instructions

1   First, in a small bowl, whisk the vinegar with the lemon juice, celery seeds, mustard and half of the garlic. Gradually whisk in 1/4 cup of the olive oil and the almond oil until emulsified. Season the dressing with salt and pepper.

2   In a mini food processor, combine the remaining garlic with the parsley, celery leaves and almonds and pulse until finely chopped. Add another 1/4 cup of of the olive oil and puree to a chunky paste. Season the pesto with salt and pepper.

3   Light a grill. Brush the mushrooms with oil and season with salt and pepper. Grill over high heat, turning once, until tender and browned, about 5 minutes. In a bowl, toss the grapes with the remaining 1 tbsp of olive oil and season with salt and pepper. Grill over high heat until the skins begin to blacken in spots, about 3 minutes; line the grill with perforated foil if the grapes will fall through. Transfer the grapes and mushrooms to a large bowl and toss with the pesto.

4   Arrange the lettuce leaves on a platter and drizzle with half of the dressing. Spoon the mushroom-and-grape salad onto the lettuce. Toss the celery with the remaining dressing, spoon it on top and serve.

WATERCRESS SALAD WITH VERJUS VINAIGRETTE

Prep Time: 15 Minutes

Cook Time: 0 Minutes

Total Time: 15 Minutes

Serve: 4

Ingredients

- 1/4 cup of verjus (see Note)
- 1/4 cup of canola oil
- Salt and freshly ground black pepper
- 2 Belgian endives, sliced crosswise
- 1 inch thick 1 bunch watercress, thick stems discarded
- 1 cup of halved green grapes
- 1/2 cup of salted marcona almonds

Instructions

- 1 In a large bowl, whisk the verjus with the canola oil and season with salt and freshly ground pepper.
- Add the sliced endives, watercress, halved grapes and almonds; toss to coat and serve.

PEAR AND ARUGULA SALAD WITH GOAT CHEESE

Prep Time: 20 Minutes

Cook Time: 0 Minutes

Total Time: 20 Minutes

Serve: 10

Ingredients

- 1/4 cup of extra-virgin olive oil
- 2 tbsp fresh lemon juice
- 1 tsp of honey
- 1/2 tsp of chopped thyme
- Salt and freshly ground pepper
- 5 ounces of baby arugula
- 3 Asian pears (about 1 1/2 pounds) peeled, cored, and thinly sliced with a mandoline; cores thrown away.
- 1/2 cup of of salted roasted pumpkin seeds
- 3 ounces of fresh goat cheese, crumbled
- Sea salt, for sprinkling

Instructions

1   First, in a small bowl, mix the lemon juice, honey, and chopped thyme with the olive oil. Add salt and pepper to the salad dressing.
2   Mix the arugula, pear slices, and pumpkin seeds in a large bowl.
3   Mix in the dressing well.

4   Crumble the goat cheese on top, sprinkle a little sea salt on top, and serve right away.

PASTA SALAD

GARDEN PESTO PASTA SALAD

Prep Time: 15 Minutes

Cook Time: 0 Minutes

Refrigerate Time: 60 Minutes

Total Time: 1 Hour 15 Minutes

Serve: 10

Ingredients

- 1 medium zucchini, halved and sliced
- 1 medium sweet red pepper, chopped
- 1 medium tomato, seeded and chopped
- 1/2 cup of grated Parmesan cheese
- 3 tbsp white wine vinegar
- 1/2 tsp salt
- 1/4 tsp pepper
- 1/4 cup of olive oil
- 1 small red onion, thinly sliced
- 1 tbsp lemon juice
- 3 cups of or 9 ounce of uncooked spiral pasta

Instructions

1. First, cook the pasta according to the package directions, then drain.
2. Drain thoroughly after rinsing with cold water.
3. Meanwhile, combine the pesto, vinegar, lemon juice, salt, and pepper in a mixing bowl.
4. Whisk in the oil gradually until combined.

5. Combine the vegetables and the pasta.

6. Drizzle pesto dressing over the salad and toss to coat.

7. Refrigerate until cold, about 1 hour, covered.

8. Garnish with Parmesan cheese.

ALMOND-APRICOT CHICKEN SALAD

Prep Time: 20 Minutes

Cook Time: 0 Minutes

Chill Time: 20 Minutes

Total Time: 30 Minutes

Serve: 10

Ingredients

- 1 tbsp lemon juice
- 6 ounces of dried apricots, thinly sliced
- 2 tsp grated lemon zest
- 2-1/2 cups of diced cooked chicken
- 3 cups of coarsely chopped fresh broccoli
- 2 tsp Dijon mustard
- 3/4 tsp dried savory
- 1-1/2 tsp salt
- 3/4 cup of sliced almonds, toasted
- 1/2 cup of chopped green onions
- 1/2 tsp pepper
- 1 package (8 ounces) spiral pasta

* 1 cup of sour cream
* 1/2 cup of chopped celery

Instructions

1 Follow the directions on the package to cook the pasta. Add the apricots during the last 4 minutes of cooking.
2 Drain and rinse with cold water; put in a large bowl.
3 Add chicken, broccoli, onions, and celery.
4 Mix the next 8 ingredients together in a small bowl.
5 Now, pour the dressing all over the salad and toss to coat.
6 Cover and chill until ready to serve. Mix in the almonds.

VERMICELLI PASTA SALAD

Prep Time: 20 Minutes

Cook Time: 0 Minutes

Chill Time: 60 Minutes

Total Time: 1 Hour 20 Minutes

Serve: 10

Ingredients

* 1 small sweet red pepper, chopped
* 1 tsp poppy seeds
* 1 bottle (16 ounces) of creamy Italian salad dressing
* 1 tsp dill seed

- 6 green onions, chopped
- 1 small green pepper, chopped
- 1 tsp caraway seeds
- 12 ounces uncooked vermicelli

Instructions

1 Cook vermicelli according to package directions.
2 Drain; transfer to a large bowl.
3 Add remaining ingredients; toss to coat.
4 Refrigerate until cold.

FRESH SUMMER PASTA SALAD

Prep Time: 20 Minutes

Cook Time: 0 Minutes

Refrigerate Time: 3 Hours

Total Time: 3 Hours 20 Minutes

Serve: 12

Ingredients

- 2 medium peaches, chopped
- 1/2 tsp salt
- 1/2 cup of fresh broccoli florets, chopped
- 1/2 cup of julienned cucumber
- 2 medium carrots, finely chopped
- 1/2 tsp pepper

- 1/2 cup of sliced celery
- 4 cups of uncooked campanelle or spiral pasta
- 1/2 cup of grated red cabbage
- 1/2 cup of julienned zucchini
- 2 cups of Caesar salad dressing
- 1 pouch (11 ounces) of light tuna in water

Instructions

- For al dente, cook the pasta according to the directions on the package.
- Drain; wash with cold water and drain well.
- Put in a large bowl.
- Add salt and pepper, carrots, peaches, tuna, celery, cucumber, zucchini, broccoli, cabbage, and tuna.
- Now, pour on the dressing and toss to coat. Cover and put in the fridge for at least 3 hours before serving.

TRI-COLOR PASTA SALAD

Prep Time: 20 Minutes

Cook Time: 0 Minutes

Chill Time: 10 Minutes

Total Time: 30 Minutes

Serve: 14

Ingredients

- 1-1/2 cups of Italian salad dressing with roasted red pepper and Parmesan
- 4 cups of fresh broccoli florets
- 1 can (6 ounces) of pitted ripe olives, drained
- 1/8 tsp salt
- 1 package (12 ounces) of tricolor spiral pasta
- 1-pint grape tomatoes
- 1/8 tsp pepper

Instructions

1. First, cook the pasta in a Dutch oven according to the directions on the package. About 2 minutes before the pasta is done, add the broccoli.
2. Drain and rinse under cold running water.
3. Transfer to a large mixing bowl.
4. Combine the tomatoes, olives, salt, and pepper in a mixing bowl.
5. Toss salad with the salad dressing to coat.
6. Chill until ready to serve.

TURKEY RAMEN NOODLE SALAD

Prep Time: 20 Minutes

Cook Time: 0 Minutes

Chill Time: 0 Minutes

Total Time: 20 Minutes

Serve: 6

Ingredients

- *1 pound sliced deli turkey, chopped*
- 1/2 cup of sliced almonds, toasted
- Thinly sliced green onions, optional
- 1 package (14 ounces) of coleslaw mix
- 6 ounces of Oriental ramen noodles
- 1/4 cup of sesame seeds
- 3 tbsp sugar
- 1/2 tsp pepper
- 1/3 cup of white wine vinegar
- 1/4 cup of canola oil

Instructions

1. Whisk the vinegar, oil, sugar, pepper, and the contents of the ramen noodle seasoning packets in a small bowl until they are all mixed together.
2. Break up the noodles and put them in a big bowl.
3. Add turkey and coleslaw mix.
4. Pour dressing on top and toss to coat.
5. Almonds and sesame seeds can be used as a topping.
6. If you want, you can put green onions on top.
7. Serve right away.

TORTELLINI CAESAR SALAD

Prep Time: 20 Minutes

Cook Time: 0 Minutes

Chill Time: 0 Minutes

Total Time: 20 Minutes

Serve: 10

Ingredients

- 1 cup of seasoned salad croutons
- 2 garlic cloves, minced
- 1/2 cup of mayonnaise
- 2 tbsp lemon juice
- 1/4 cup of 2% milk
- 1 package (19 ounces) of frozen cheese tortellini
- 8 cups of torn romaine
- 1/4 cup of plus 1/3 cup of shredded Parmesan cheese
- Halved cherry tomatoes, optional

Instructions

1   Follow the directions on the package to cook the tortellini.
2   In the meantime, mix the mayonnaise, milk, 1/4 cup of Parmesan cheese, lemon juice, and garlic in a small bowl.
3   Drain and rinse the tortellini in cold water, then put them in a large bowl.
4   Add the rest of the romaine and Parmesan.

5   Drizzle the salad with the dressing right before serving and toss
     to coat.

6   If you want, you can add croutons and tomatoes on top.

SESAME ALMOND SLAW

Prep Time: 20 Minutes

Cook Time: 0 Minutes

Chill Time: 0 Minutes

Total Time: 20 Minutes

Serve: 2

Ingredients

- 2 tsp sesame seeds, toasted
- Dash salt
- 3/4 cup of shredded cabbage
- 2 tsp slivered almonds, toasted
- 1 package (3 ounces) of ramen noodles
- 3/4 cup of shredded romaine
- 1/2 tsp sesame oil
- 1-1/2 tsp sugar
- 2 tbsp sliced green onion
- 1 tsp water
- 1/4 tsp of reduced-sodium soy sauce
- 1-1/2 tsp canola oil
- Dash pepper

- 1 tbsp rice vinegar

Instructions

1. Cut ramen noodles in half and save half of the noodles and the seasoning for another meal.
2. Break up the rest of the noodles and put them in a bowl.
3. Put in the cabbage, romaine, onion, almonds, and sesame seeds.
4. For the dressing, put the vinegar, sugar, canola oil, water, sesame oil, soy sauce, salt, and pepper in a jar with a fitting lid. Shake the jar well.
5. Mix the salad with the dressing.
6. Serve right away.

LEMONY TORTELLINI BACON SALAD

Prep Time: 20 Minutes

Cook Time: 0 Minutes

Chill Time: 0 Minutes

Total Time: 20 Minutes

Serve: 4

Ingredients

- 3/4 cup of mayonnaise
- 2 tsp lemon juice
- 1/4 tsp salt

- 4 bacon strips, cooked and crumbled
- 2 cups of or 8 ounces of frozen cheese tortellini
- 1 tbsp balsamic vinegar
- 3/4 tsp dried oregano
- 5 ounces of spring mix salad greens
- 4 cups of fresh broccoli florets

Instructions

1. Follow the directions on the package to cook the tortellini in a large saucepan. Add the broccoli during the last 5 minutes of cooking.
2. In the meantime, mix the mayo, vinegar, lemon juice, oregano, and salt in a small bowl.
3. Drain the tortellini and broccoli, and then use cold water to gently rinse them.
4. Put the food in a large bowl.
5. Mix the salad with the dressing.
6. Sprinkle bacon over salad greens and serve.

CUCUMBER SHELL SALAD

Prep Time: 20 Minutes

Cook Time: 0 Minutes

Chill Time: 2 Hours

Total Time: 2 Hours 20 Minutes

Serve: 16

Ingredients

- 1 package (16 ounces) of medium pasta shells
- 1 medium cucumber, halved and sliced
- 1 small red onion, chopped
- 1 cup of ranch salad dressing

Instructions

1. Follow the directions on the package to cook the pasta, then drain it and rinse it in cold water.
2. Mix the pasta, peas, cucumber, and onion together in a large bowl.
3. Mix the salad with the dressing.
4. Cover and chill for at least 2 hours before serving.

CORN PASTA SALAD

Prep Time: 20 Minutes

Cook Time: 0 Minutes

Refrigerate Time: 8-12 Hours

Total Time: 8-12 Hours 20 Minutes

Serve: 10

Ingredients

- 2 cups of cooked tricolor spiral pasta
- 1 package (16 ounces) of frozen corn, thawed
- 1 cup of chopped celery
- 1 medium green pepper, chopped
- 1 cup of chopped seeded tomatoes
- 1/2 cup of diced pimientos
- 1/2 cup of chopped red onion
- 1 cup of picante sauce
- 2 tbsp canola oil
- 1 tbsp lemon juice
- 1 garlic clove, minced
- 1 tbsp sugar
- 1/2 tsp salt

Instructions

1. Combine the first 7 ingredients in a large mixing bowl.
2. Combine the picante sauce, oil, lemon juice, garlic, sugar, and salt in a jar with a tightfitting lid; shake well.
3. Toss the pasta mixture with the sauce to coat.

4   Refrigerate overnight, covered.

WAGON WHEEL PASTA SALAD

Prep Time: 20 Minutes

Cook Time: 0 Minutes

Refrigerate Time: 2 Hours

Total Time: 2 Hours 20 Minutes

Serve: 16

Ingredients

- 1 cup of halved cherry tomatoes
- 1 cup of mayonnaise
- 1 tsp salt
- 3 cups of uncooked wagon wheel pasta or elbow macaroni
- 1/2 cup of picante sauce
- 1/2 cup of thinly sliced green onions
- 1 small green pepper, julienned
- 1 cup of cubed cheddar cheese
- 1 can (16 ounces) of kidney beans, rinsed and drained
- 1 tsp ground cumin

Instructions

1   First, cook the pasta according to the package directions, then drain and rinse in cold water.

2   Combine the pasta, beans, cheese, tomatoes, peppers, and onions in a large mixing bowl.

3   Combine the mayonnaise, picante sauce, salt, and cumin in a bowl; pour over the salad and toss to coat.

4   Refrigerate for 2 hours before serving, covered.

NUTTY BROCCOLI SLAW

Prep Time: 20 Minutes

Cook Time: 0 Minutes

Chill Time: 0 Minutes

Total Time: 20 Minutes

Serve: 16

Ingredients

- 2 cups of sliced green onions (about 2 bunches)
- 1/2 cup of olive oil
- 1 package (16 ounces) broccoli coleslaw mix
- 1-1/2 cups of broccoli florets
- 1/2 cup of slivered almonds, toasted
- 1/2 cup of sugar
- 1/2 cup of cider vinegar
- 1 package (3 ounces) of chicken ramen noodles
- 1 cup of sunflower kernels, toasted
- 6 ounces of ripe olives, drained and halved

Instructions

1   Set aside the noodle seasoning packet; in a large mixing bowl, crush the noodles.

2   Combine the slaw mix, onions, broccoli, olives, sunflower kernels, and almonds in a mixing bowl.

3   Combine the sugar, vinegar, oil, and seasoning packet contents in a jar with a tight-fitting lid; shake well.

4   Toss salad with dressing to coat.

5   Serve right away.

HEARTY SIX-LAYER PASTA SALAD

Prep Time: 20 Minutes

Cook Time: 0 Minutes

Refrigerate Time: 8-12 Hours

Total Time: 8-12 Hours 20 Minutes

Serve: 12

Ingredients

- 1/8 tsp pepper
- 1 cup of of shredded Colby or Monterey Jack cheese
- 1/4 tsp salt

dressing

- 2 tbsp minced fresh parsley
- 3 cups of shredded lettuce
- 3 large hard-boiled eggs, sliced
- 1-1/2 cups of uncooked small pasta shells

- 1 package (10 ounces) of frozen peas, thawed
- 1 cup of mayonnaise

Toppings

- 2 tsp Dijon mustard
- 2 green onions, chopped
- 2 cups of shredded cooked chicken breast
- 1/4 cup of sour cream
- 1 tbsp canola oil

Instructions

1 First, cook pasta as directed on the package; drain and rinse with cold water.
2 To coat, drizzle with oil and toss.
3 Fill a 2-1/2-quart glass serving bowl halfway with lettuce; top with pasta and eggs.
4 Season with salt and pepper to taste. Layer chicken and peas on top.
5 Mix dressing ingredients in a small bowl until well combined; spread over the top.
6 Refrigerate for several hours or overnight, covered.
7 Sprinkle with cheese and parsley just before serving.

CHILLED SOBA NOODLE SALAD WITH YUZU DRESSING

Prep Time: 30 Minutes

Cook Time: 0 Minutes

Chill Time: 0 Minutes

Total Time: 30 Minutes

Serve: 4

Ingredients

- For the Yuzu Dressing:
- 1 tbsp toasted sesame oil
- 1 clove garlic, grated
- ½ tbsp Chinese sesame paste
- ½ tbsp ponzu
- ½ inch thin piece of peeled fresh ginger, grated
- 4 ¼ tbsp Korean yuzu tea

Salt

- 1 tbsp water
- ½ tsp yuzu kosho
- 2 tbsp extra-virgin olive oil
- 3 ½ tbsp apple cider vinegar

For the Soba Salad

- 1 small head of romaine lettuce, very thinly sliced
- 1 cup of pea shoots or watercress sprouts
- 2 medium carrots, peeled and thinly sliced
- 14 ounces of soba noodles

- Couple of pinches of salt and sugar
- 1 cup of wonton crisps
- ½ radicchio, cored and very thinly sliced
- 1 cup of cherry tomatoes, quartered
- 1 cup of drained canned mandarin orange segments
- 2 Persian cucumbers, cut into ¼-inch slices

Instructions

Prepare the yuzu dressing

1. In a blender or small food processor, mix the yuzu tea, vinegar, water, sesame oil, olive oil, ponzu, sesame paste, yuzu koshu, ginger, and garlic. Blend until it's smooth. Use salt to season to taste.

Prepare the salad

1. In a medium bowl, combine cucumbers, salt, and sugar, and rub the seasonings into the cucumbers. Allow to stand at room temperature for 30 minutes while you prepare the remaining vegetables.
2. Now, cook the soba noodles according to the package directions, stirring the pot every 30 seconds to prevent clumping. Make an ice water bowl. Drain the noodles and place them in a bowl of ice water to cool. Drain and set aside the noodles.
3. Mix the romaine and radicchio with a few spoonfuls of dressing in a big bowl, then divide the salad among four wide, shallow bowls. In the middle of each bowl, swirl a portion of soba noodles. Place the cucumbers, tomatoes, carrots, orange segments, sprouts, and wonton crisps in neat piles around the soba. Serve each serving with a few spoonfuls of dressing on top.

GREENS PASTA SALAD

Prep Time: 40 Minutes

Cook Time: 5 Minutes

Chill Time: 30 Minutes

Total Time: 1 Hour 15 Minutes

Serve: 8

Ingredients

- 1/2 cup of mayonnaise
- 1 pound asparagus, cut into 1-inch
- Freshly ground black pepper
- Kosher salt and ice
- 1 pound campanelle pasta
- 1/2 pound arugula, thick stems discarded, leaves coarsely chopped
- 1 large garlic clove, grated
- 1 cup of buttermilk
- 2 cups of peas, fresh or frozen
- 2 tbsp Champagne vinegar

Instructions

1. First, fill a large pot with water and bring it to a boil. Add a lot of salt to the water.
2. Now, cook the pasta until it is "al dente." Drain well, then put in a big bowl.

3. Whisk the buttermilk, mayonnaise, vinegar, and garlic together in a medium bowl.

4. Add salt and pepper to taste. Toss the warm pasta with half of the dressing and let it cool for 30 minutes.

5. Now, fill the pot with water and bring it back to a boil. Add a lot of salt to the water. Put together an ice bath.

6. Put the asparagus and peas in the boiling water and cook for about 2 minutes or until they are crisp-tender.

7. Drain the vegetables and put them in the ice bath to cool down completely. Drain the vegetables well.

8. Stir the remaining dressing, asparagus, and peas into the pasta.

9. Salt and pepper the dish, then add the arugula and serve.

PASTA SALAD WITH FETA AND HERBS

Prep Time: 25 Minutes

Cook Time: 0 Minutes

Chill Time: 0 Minutes

Total Time: 25 Minutes

Serve: 8

Ingredients

- 5 ounces of feta cheese, crumbled (about 1 1/4 cups)
- 1 tsp grated garlic
- 1/2 cup of buttermilk
- 3/4 cup of salted roasted sunflower seed kernels

- 4 cups of of torn mixed tender fresh herbs (such as basil, mint, dill, and chives)
- 1 1/2 cups of of thinly sliced celery
- 1/2 tsp black pepper
- 1 tbsp of grated lemon zest plus 1/4 cup of fresh lemon juice
- 1 pound uncooked penne pasta
- 1 1/2 tsp kosher salt
- 1 cup of cherry tomatoes, halved
- 1/4 cup of mayonnaise
- 2 tbsp Louisiana-style hot sauce
- 1/2 red onion, cut in half lengthwise and thinly sliced

Instructions

1. Follow the directions on the package to cook the pasta.
2. Drain the pasta and rinse it well under cold running water.
3. While the pasta is cooking, mix the feta, buttermilk, mayonnaise, hot sauce, lemon zest and juice, salt, garlic, and black pepper in a medium bowl.
4. Put the pasta in a large bowl to serve.
5. Mix in torn herbs, buttermilk dressing, celery, tomatoes, red onion, and sunflower seeds.

PASTA SALAD WITH ARUGULA, TOMATOES, PINE NUTS, AND HERB DRESSING

Prep Time: 25 Minutes

Cook Time: 0 Minutes

Chill Time: 0 Minutes

Total Time: 25 Minutes

Serve: 4

Ingredients

- Kosher salt and freshly ground black pepper
- 1/2 cup of basil leaves
- 1/2 small red onion, cut into small dice
- 1/4 cup of mayonnaise
- 1 1/4 cups of grape tomatoes, halved
- 1/4 cup of extra-virgin olive oil
- 1/4 cup of plus 3 tbsp pine nuts
- 1/2 cup of cilantro leaves
- 1 1/2 tbsp fresh lemon juice
- 2 1/2 cups of baby arugula
- 1 pound fusilli pasta and 1 garlic clove
- 2 tsp coarsely chopped oregano leaves

Instructions

1   Turn the oven on to 350°. Toast 3 tbsp of pine nuts in a pie plate
    for about 5 minutes, or until they are golden and smell good. Set
    aside to cool.

2   Now, cook the fusilli in a large pot of salted water that is boiling
    until it is "al dente."

3   Rinse the pasta under cold water, drain it again, and put it in a
    large bowl.

4   In the meantime, chop the cilantro, basil, oregano, and garlic
    together in a food processor until they are in large pieces.

5   Add the rest of the 1/4 cup of pine nuts, mayonnaise, olive oil,
    and lemon juice, and process until smooth.

6   Add salt and pepper to the herb dressing.

7   Mix the toasted pine nuts, arugula, tomatoes, red onion, and
    herb dressing with the fusilli.

8   Salt and pepper the pasta salad, then serve.

ESQUITES-STYLE POBLANO PASTA SALAD

Prep Time: 10 Minutes

Cook Time: 20 Minutes

Chill Time: 30 Minutes

Total Time: 1 Hour

Serve: 8

Ingredients

- ¼ cup of plus 2 tbsp crema Mexicana

- 2 tbsp chopped fresh cilantro, more cilantro leaves for garnish
- 6 cups of fresh yellow corn kernels
- 12 ounces uncooked orecchiette pasta
- 1 garlic clove, grated using a Microplane grater
- 3 tbsp vegetable oil, divided
- 2 ounces of Cotija cheese, crumbled (about 1/2 cup of), divided
- 2 tbsp extra-virgin olive oil
- 4 ounces of bunch scallions, root ends, and dark green parts trimmed
- 4 tsp of kosher salt, divided, or more for seasoning
- 1 medium zucchini, thinly sliced crosswise (1 1/2 cups)
- ¼ cup of plus 2 tbsp mayonnaise
- ½ tsp of ancho chile powder, plus more for garnish
- 1 tsp of freshly ground black pepper, plus more for garnish
- 1 medium-size poblano chile, stemmed, seeded, and finely chopped (about 2/3 cup) 1 tsp of grated lime zest plus 2 tbsp of juice

Instructions

1. Follow the directions on the package to cook the pasta. Drain and put away.
2. In the meantime, heat 2 tbsp of the vegetable oil on medium-high in a large cast-iron skillet. Add the corn and cook, stirring every so often, for 8 to 10 minutes, until the kernels are lightly charred and soft.
3. Put the corn in a big bowl. Wipe skillet clean. Add scallions to the skillet and cook over medium-high heat, turning them every so often, for about 4 minutes or until they are lightly charred. Place

the scallions on a cutting board and slice them thinly in a crosswise direction. In a bowl, add scallions to the corn.

4   Add the last tbsp of vegetable oil and turn the heat down to medium.

5   Add the zucchini and poblano and cook, stirring every so often, for about 5 minutes, until the vegetables are soft and some spots are brown.

6   Add the zucchini, poblano, orecchiette, olive oil, black pepper, ancho chile powder, and 3 1/4 tsp of salt to the bowl with the corn mixture. Mix by tossing.

7   Let the mixture cool at room temperature for about 30 minutes. (You can put the cooled corn mixture in the fridge for an hour or up to 12 hours and serve it cold if you want.

8   If you want, you can add salt before going on.)

9   In a small bowl, mix the remaining 3/4 tsp of salt with the crema, mayonnaise, chopped cilantro, lime zest and juice, garlic, and cilantro.

10 Put the corn mixture in a big bowl or on a large plate. Pour 1/4 cup of of the crema mixture on top and sprinkle with 3 or 4 grinds of black pepper and some ancho chile powder.

11 For decoration, add 1/4 cup of of the Cotija and a few cilantro leaves.

12 Serve the pasta salad with the remaining 12 cups of the crema mixture and 14 cups of the Cotija on top to drizzle and sprinkle.

PASTA SALAD WITH GRILLED VEGETABLES, PARSLEY, AND FETA

Prep Time: 25 Minutes

Cook Time: 0 Minutes

Chill Time: 0 Minutes

Total Time: 25 Minutes

Serve: 8

Ingredients

- 1 cup of parsley leaves, coarsely chopped
- 4 ounces French feta cheese, crumbled
- 1/2 pound thin asparagus and ground pepper
- 1/3 cup of pitted kalamata olives, chopped
- 2 1/2 tbsp fresh lemon juice
- Kosher salt and 1 medium zucchini, sliced
- 1 small shallot, finely chopped
- 7 tbsp extra-virgin olive oil
- 3/4 pound orecchiette and 1/2 small eggplant, sliced

Instructions

1   Start a grill or grill pan on high heat. Cook the orecchiette until it is al dente in a pot of salted water that is boiling. The pasta should be drained, rinsed in cold water, and drained well. The orecchiette should be put in a big bowl.

2   In the meantime, season the asparagus, zucchini, and eggplant with salt and pepper and brush them with 2 tbsp of olive oil. Turn the asparagus several times until it is crisptender and charred, which takes about 2 minutes. Turn the zucchini once until it is

tender and charred, which takes about 3 minutes. Turn the eggplant once until it is tender and charred, which takes about 5 minutes.

3	Move the vegetables from the grill to a work surface. Cut the asparagus into pieces that are 1 inch long. Cut the zucchini into 1/2-inch-wide pieces across its length. Cut the eggplant slices in half along their length, then cut them into 1/2-inch pieces across. Mix the vegetables that were grilled with the orecchiette.

4	Whisk the lemon juice, shallot, and the last 5 tbsp of olive oil together in a small bowl. Pour the dressing over the pasta and stir to coat. Add the feta cheese, parsley, and olives. Season with salt and pepper, toss again, and then serve.

CHICKEN SALAD

POPCORN CHICKEN SALAD

Prep Time: 30 Minutes

Total Times: 30 Minutes

Serving: 4

Ingredients

- 4 scallions, sliced
- 1 medium cucumber, about 10½ ounces/298 grams
- 8 tbsp honey mustard dressing
- 4 tbsp sunflower seeds, roasted (no shells)
- 8 cups of baby lettuce mix
- 1 pound popcorn chicken 454 grams
- 1 cup of microgreens
- 10-12 small radishes, about 12 ounces/340 grams
- 4 ounces feta, crumbled 113 grams
- 5 ounces roasted red peppers, sliced 142 grams (from a jar)

Instructions

1. Follow the directions on the box to cook the popcorn chicken. (See the article above for Ninja Foodi, oven, or microwave directions.)
2. Cut the cucumber into small pieces, the radishes and scallions into thin slices, and the roasted red peppers into thin strips.
3. Split the baby lettuce among four salad bowls or containers for meal prep.

4   On top of each salad, put a quarter of the baked popcorn chicken, microgreens, cucumber, roasted red pepper, scallions, radish, feta, and sunflower seeds.

5   Before serving the salads, drizzle them with honey mustard salad dressing. Enjoy!

LMON BASIL CHICKEN SALAD

Prep Time: 25 Minutes

Total Times: 25 Minutes

Serving: 6

Ingredients

For The Chicken Salad

- 2 shallots or ½ onion (any color)
- 4 bell pepper any color
- 2 cloves garlic
- 2 lbs. rotisserie chicken yields 4 cups
- ½ cup of basil plus more for garnish

For The Lemon Mayo Dressing

- ⅛ tsp. Kosher salt adjusts to taste
- ⅓ cup of mayo
- ⅛ tsp. pepper adjust to taste
- 3 Tbsp. lemon juice

- 2 Tbsp. Dijon mustard optional: gluten-free bread, wraps, or crackers to serve

Instructions

For the salad with chicken

1. Chop up 4 garlic cloves and 2 shallots (or half an onion).
2. Dice 1 large bell pepper (any color).
3. Chop up 1/2 cup of fresh basil.
4. When the rotisserie chicken is cool enough to touch, remove it from the package, peel off the skin, and throw it away. Pull the white and dark meat carefully off the bones and put it on a cutting board. Throw away the bones.
5. You can cube or shred the pieces of rotisserie chicken. You can cut the pieces into any size you want. Dice the chicken and put it in a large bowl.
6. Put the chopped chicken, minced garlic, shallots, and peppers in the mixing bowl.

For the Lemon Mayonnaise Dressing

1. In a small bowl, mix 1/3 cup of mayonnaise, 2 tbsp of Dijon mustard, 3 tbsp of lemon juice, and 1/8 tsp each of kosher salt and pepper. Stir until everything is well mixed.
2. Pour as much or as little dressing as you want over the chicken salad. Stir until everything is well mixed.
3. Mix the chopped basil into the chicken salad until it is all mixed in.
4. Serve in a full or half sandwich, wrap, tortilla, pita bread, naan bread, lettuce wrap, or with crackers. (If you have gluten-related concerns, ensure the brand you select is glutenfree.)

5   Squeeze a lemon wedge over the top and sprinkle more basil on top. Adjust salt and pepper levels as needed (optional).

RADICCHIO ENDIVE CHICKEN SALAD

Prep Time: 10 Minutes

Cook Time: 10 Minutes

Total Times: 20 Minutes

Serving: 6

Ingredients

- 1 Cup of basil leaves fresh
- 1/2 Cup of parmesan shaved (dairy free or regular)
- 2 chicken breasts boneless skinless
- 1/2 Tsp. paprika
- 3 Heads radicchio
- 3 Heads endive
- 1/2 Tsp. black pepper
- 1 Hearts romaine lettuce
- 1 Cup of cherry tomatoes
- 1 Tsp. onion powder

Dressing

- 2 Tbsp. mayonnaise
- 1 Tbsp. Honey
- 1/4 Cup of olive oil
- 1/4 Cup of red wine vinegar
- 1 Tbsp. shallot minced
- 1 Tbsp. yellow mustard
- 2 lemons juiced

- 1/4 Cup of mustard whole grain
- 3 Cloves garlic

Instructions

1. Pound the chicken until it is 1/2 inch thick. Add black pepper, onion powder, and paprika to both sides of a chicken breast. For 5 minutes, heat a grill pan made of cast iron over high heat.

2. Add the chicken and cook each side for 4 minutes. Put the meat on a wooden cutting board and cut it into pieces that are easy to eat.

3. Wash your food. Mix the grilled chicken with the radicchio, endives, romaine, tomatoes, basil, and parmesan in a large bowl. Radicchio and endives should be cut into fourths. Cut romaine hearts in half, and then each half in half again.

4. Combine all the dressing ingredients in a blender or food processor for 15 seconds. Use half of the resulting dressing to dress the salad, tossing it to coat thoroughly. You can keep the remaining dressing on the side to enjoy later.

AIR FRYER BLACKENED CHICKEN CAESAR SALAD

Prep Time: 15 Minutes

Cook Time: 27 Minutes

Total Times: 42 Minutes

Serving: 6

Ingredients

Blackened Chicken

- 1/2 Tbsp. smoked paprika
- 1/2 Tsp. cayenne pepper
- 1 Tsp. cumin
- 1 Tsp. chili powder
- 1 Tsp. black pepper freshly cracked
- 1/2 Tsp. onion powder
- 1 Tsp. thyme
- 2 romaine hearts
- 1/2 cup of parmesan cheese shredded
- 2 chicken breasts boneless skinless
- 1 Tbsp. grapeseed oil
- 1 Tsp. sea salt
- 1 Tsp. garlic powder

Caesar Dressing

- 1 egg yolk
- 3 anchovies
- 2 Tsp. Dijon mustard
- 1 Pinch of black pepper
- 1 Lemon juiced
- 4 Cloves garlic
- 1 Tsp. Worcheshire sauce
- 1/2 cup of parmesan cheese grated
- 1/3 Cup of grapeseed oil
- 1 Pinch salt

Homemade Air Fryer Croutons

- 1/2 Tbsp. garlic powder
- 1 1/2 Tbsp. Italian seasoning

- 4 Tbsp. olive oil extra virgin
- 1/2 Loaf white bread
- 1 Tsp. salt

Instructions

1 Rub grapeseed oil on both sides of the chicken breast.

2 Combine the blackened seasoning. Rub each side of the chicken generously. Allow the chicken to sit in the blackened rub for 15 minutes. While you're waiting, make some croutons.

3 Cut the bread into 1" cubes. Combine in a large mixing bowl. Over the bread, drizzle with olive oil and season with garlic powder, Italian seasoning, and salt. To coat, toss with a fork. Before adding the bread, preheat the air fryer to 360°F for 5 minutes. Once it has reached the desired temperature, put the bread in the air fryer and apply a light coating of canola oil spray.

4 Cook for 7 minutes, shaking the basket halfway through. Take out and set aside.

5 Warm up the air fryer for 5 minutes at 370°F.

6 Fill the air fryer basket halfway with the chicken. Cook for 10 minutes, then flip and cook for another 10 minutes. Make strips out of it.

7 Add 1" piece of romaine lettuce to a salad bowl.

8 Make the Caesar dressing. In a food processor or blender, pure all ingredients except the grapeseed oil for 5 seconds. Puree for 5 seconds after adding 12 of the oil. Puree the remaining oil for 15 seconds.

9 Dress the salad with Caesar dressing. Toss in the shredded parmesan and croutons. Serve with blackened chicken strips on top.

CURRIED CHICKEN SALAD

Prep Time: 20 Minutes

Total Times: 20 Minutes

Serving: 4

Ingredients

For the chicken salad

- ½ cup of roasted and salted pistachios (shells removed)
- 3 scallions, thinly sliced
- ½ cup of chopped Italian parsley
- ½ cup of golden raisins, plus more to taste
- 3 stalks celery, small-diced
- 2 medium/large cooked chicken breasts, shredded
- ½ cup of roasted cashews, plus more to taste

Honey curry dressing

- Salt and pepper to taste
- 1 to 2 tbsp honey - plus more to taste
- 1 cup of Greek yogurt
- 1 tbsp yellow curry powder
- ½ tsp garlic powder
- Fresh lemon juice to taste

Instructions

1 To make the honey curry dressing, follow these steps: In a mixing bowl, combine the Greek yogurt, curry powder, honey, and garlic powder. Then, to taste, add the freshly squeezed lemon juice.

Season to taste with salt and pepper. If more sweetness is desired, add more honey. Squeeze a little more lemon juice for more acidity.

2   Combine the shredded chicken, celery, cashews, raisins, pistachios, scallions, and Italian parsley in a large mixing bowl with the prepared honey curry dressing. If necessary, season with additional salt and pepper.

3   Serve and have fun! I like to serve it with a bed of mixed greens. Sandwiches and wraps can also be made.

ROTISSERIE CHICKEN SALAD

Prep Time: 20 Minutes

Cook Time: 10 Minutes

Total Times: 30 Minutes

Serving: 4

Ingredients

Salad

- 80 g mixed leaves
- 2 eggs, room temperature
- 1 chicken, rotisserie
- 1 avocado, small
- 3 slices bread
- 1 tbsp olive oil
- 1 carrot

- 1 tsp garlic powder
- 12 cherry tomatoes

Salad Dressing

- 1 tbsp tahini
- ¼ cup of water
- 1 tbsp sour cream
- ½ lemon
- 1 cup of parsley, chopped

Instructions

Salad

1. Preheat the oven to 180° Celsius. (350 degrees Fahrenheit).
2. Cut each slice of bread into 9-12 squares. On top, drizzle 1 tbsp olive oil and 1 tsp garlic powder. Bake the bread for 10-15 minutes on a baking sheet-lined dish.
3. Remove and set aside the chicken wings. Remove the skin from the chicken breast and cut it into pieces. Remove all the other meat and shred it into thin pieces with your hands.
4. Wash and dry the mixed leaves before storing them.
5. Cut the avocado into cubes.
6. Remove the skin from the carrot. Using a Y peeler, peel wide strips. Roll 6-8 of the bestlooking strips into ribbons.
7. Cut the cherry tomatoes in half.
8. A small pot of water should be brought to a boil. After slowly submerging two roomtemperature eggs into the water with a spoon, bring to a boil for 5 minutes. Remove the eggs and place them in ice water to stop cooking.

Salad Dressings

1 1 cup of chopped parsley is required.

2 Combine parsley, tahini, 12 lemon juice, water, and sour cream in a food processor.

3 Blitz everything until everything is well combined.

Assembly

1 In a medium mixing bowl, combine the mixed leaves and carrot strips (not the ribbons) and arrange them on a platter.

2 Arrange the shredded chicken, avocado, and cherry tomatoes in this order on the platter.

3 Carrot ribbons should be inserted between the leaves.

4 Croutons are not required.

5 Place two sliced chicken breasts on top, then two wings on the side.

6 After peeling the eggs, slice them in half before adding them to the salad

7 Drizzle with green tahini dressing on top.

8 Season with salt and pepper to taste.Serve.

LOW-CARB CHICKEN SALAD, NO MAYO

Prep Time: 15 Minutes

Cook Time: 30 Minutes

Total Times: 45 Minutes

Serving: 4

Ingredients

Salad

- ¼ cup of Greek yogurt
- 80 g baby spinach
- 1 tbsp olive oil
- ¼ cup of macadamia nuts
- 28 raspberries
- 2 chicken thighs, boneless
- ½ tsp garlic powder
- 4 radish
- 2 tbsp flat leaf parsley, chopped

Salad Dressing

- 2 tbsp apple cider vinegar
- 2 tbsp water
- 2 tbsp olive oil
- ½ cup of flat-leaf parsley, chopped
- 1 avocado
- ¼ tsp salt

Instructions

Salad

1. Preheat your oven to 180 degrees Celsius (350 degrees Fahrenheit). Then, in a small bowl, mix 1 tbsp of olive oil, 1/4 tsp of garlic powder, and salt and pepper to your taste. Coat the chicken thighs with this mixture and place them in a baking dish. Bake the chicken for 30 minutes in the preheated oven. Allow them to cool before slicing.
2. Cut two radishes into 6-8 wedges each, and thinly slice the other two.
3. Chop parsley leaves to yield 2 tbsp.

Dressing for Salad

1. Remove the avocado skin and stone and set aside.
2. Cut parsley leaves into 12-cup of pieces.
3. Combine avocado, parsley, olive oil, apple cider vinegar, water, and salt in a food processor.
4. Blitz until everything is well combined.

Assembly

1. Dollop avocado salad dressing around the edge of the platter. Join the dollops together with the back of a tsp to form a ring.
2. Top the avocado salad dressing with dollops of Greek yogurt. Make swirls with the tsp so that the white blends into the green.
3. Place a generous dollop of creamy avocado dressing and Greek yogurt in the center of the platter, followed by the swirls.
4. Top with baby spinach leaves. However, do not cover the dressing around the edges.
5. In this order, arrange the radishes, raspberries, sliced chicken thighs, and macadamia nuts.

6   As a garnish, sprinkle with chopped parsley leaves.

7   Season to taste with salt and pepper.

8   Serve.

MEXICAN CHICKEN AVOCADO SALAD

Prep Time: 15 Minutes

Cook Time: 12 Minutes

Total Times: 27 Minutes

Serving: 4

Ingredients

Cooking Chicken

- ½ tsp cumin powder
- 2 chicken breasts cut in half lengthwise
- 1 ½ tsp smoked paprika
- 1 tsp cooking oil
- 1 tsp chipotle chili powder
- salt and pepper

Salad Base

- ¼ fresh chopped cilantro
- 4 small cucumbers sliced
- 1 cup of roasted corn kernels see notes
- 4 cup of spring mix (or lettuce) or more
- 2 avocados peeled and diced
- Optional: ½ cup of cherry tomatoes sliced

Dressing

- salt and pepper
- 1 tbsp chopped cilantro
- 2 tbsp lime juice
- 3 tbsp olive oil
- 2 small garlic cloves minced

Instructions

How to cook chicken

1. Combine chipotle chili powder, smoked paprika, cumin powder, pepper, and salt in a small bowl to create the spice mix.
2. Split the chicken breasts in half vertically and season both sides with the rub.
3. Heat some cooking oil in a pan of cast iron on medium heat.
4. Cook the chicken for about 3 minutes in a single layer. Then turn the chicken over and cook for another 3 minutes or until it is well done.
5. Let it cool, and then cut it into pieces that are easy to eat.

Salad Dressing

1. Combine olive oil, lime juice, garlic, cilantro, salt, and pepper. Co in a small bowline and set aside.

Salad base

2. Put greens, diced avocado, corn kernels, cucumber, and other salad ingredients in a large bowl.
3. Then, add chicken slices and salad dressing that has already been made to the salad base. Mix everything gently with two wooden spatulas or salad hands.

MEDITERRANEAN CHICKEN SALAD

Prep Time: 20 Minutes

Cook Time: 10 Minutes

Total Times: 30 Minutes

Serving: 2

Ingredients

For the Salad

- black pepper and sea salt - to taste ⅓ cup of feta cheese – crumbled or diced
- ⅓ cup of kalamata olives – pitted and halved
- 1 cup of (200 g) cherry tomatoes – halved
- ½ avocado
- ½ tsp dried oregano
- 1 tbsp lemon juice
- ½ small red onion – finely sliced into half-moon shapes
- 2 tbsp extra virgin olive oil
- 2 cups of rocket leaves/arugula
- ⅓ cup of fresh mint leaves – finely sliced

For the Chicken

- sea salt and black pepper, to taste
- 1 tsp dried oregano
- 1 tbsp extra virgin olive oil
- 4 chicken tenderloins

Instructions

1. Put the tomatoes, olives, onion, feta, mint, and oregano that you have already prepared into a large bowl. Throw around to mix. Add sea salt, freshly ground black pepper, olive oil, and lemon juice to the salad to taste. See Note 4.

2. Next, cut off the white tendon at one end of the chicken tenderloin. Put the chicken between two sheets of cling film and gently pound it until it is an even thickness and almost twice as big.

3. Heat a grill pan or nonstick pan over medium-high heat. Olive oil should be used on both sides of the chicken. Sea salt, fresh black pepper, and dried oregano should be used as seasonings. See Note 5.

4. When the pan is ready, cook the chicken for 1 to 2 minutes per side, or until it is done all the way through, and set it aside. See Note 6.

5. Put the rocket or arugula and avocado on the plates you'll be using. Put the tomato salsa on top.

6. Cut the chicken into pieces and put them in the salad. Serve right away.

LEFTOVER ROAST CHICKEN POTATO SALAD

Prep Time: 15 Minutes

Cook Time: 3 Minutes

Total Times: 18 Minutes

Serving: 4

Ingredients

Salad

- 2 tbsp capers
- 100 g green beans
- 300 g potatoes, roasted
- 1 bunch radish
- 300 g chicken, roasted, shredded

Salad Dressing

- salt, to taste pepper, to taste
- 1 cup of Greek yogurt
- 2 cups of mixed herbs, flat-leaf parsley, basil, chives
- 1 tsp lemon zest
- 1 tbsp olive oil, extra virgin
- 1 garlic clove

Instructions

Salad

1   Shred small pieces of the roast chicken you have left over.

2   Cut any leftover roasted potatoes into pieces that are easy to eat.

3   Wash, cut in half, and trim green beans.

4   Bring a pot with about 3 quarts of water to a boil. Quickly blanch the green beans for 1 to 2 minutes.

5   Drain the green beans and run them under cold water to stop the green beans from cooking.

6   Trim radishes and wash them well.

7   Depending on the size, cut it in half or four.

Salad Dressing

1   Wash and shake dry the parsley, basil, and chives.

2   Put the parsley, basil, chives, garlic cloves, Greek yogurt, lemon zest, and extra virgin olive oil into a small food processor.

3   Mix until it's smooth.

4   Add salt and pepper to taste.

Assembly

1   Mix the roasted chicken, potatoes, green beans, and radishes together in a large bowl.

2   Spread a scoop of green goddess dressing on the bottom of a large platter.

3   Mix the green goddess dressing with the roast chicken potato salad.

4   Spread capers over the top.

5   Add tasty salt and pepper to taste before serving.

GRILLED CHEEK CHICKEN SALAD

Prep Time: 30 Minutes

Marinate Time: 2 Hours

Cook Time: 20 Minutes

Total Times: 2 Hours 50 Minutes

Serving: 4

Ingredients

For the Marinated Greek Chicken

- ½ lemon - zested
- 2 tsp fresh thyme - minced
- ½ tsp freshly cracked black pepper
- 1 tsp fresh rosemary - minced
- 3 chicken breasts - (approx. 2 pounds)
- ¼ cups of olive oil
- 2 tsp fresh oregano - minced
- 1 tsp salt
- 1 lemon – juiced
- 2 tsp fresh parsley - minced
- 3 cloves garlic – minced

For the Greek Vinaigrette

- 1 tsp Dijon mustard
- ⅓ cup of red wine vinegar
- ½ tsp fresh cracked black pepper
- ½ tsp dried oregano

- ½ tsp salt
- ¼ cup of olive oil
- 1 lemon - juiced
- 3 cloves garlic – minced

For the Salad

- 10 ounces cherry tomatoes - halved
- ½ English cucumber - sliced
- Fresh chopped dill and parsley - for serving
- ½ red bell pepper - seeded and sliced
- ½ green bell pepper - seeded and sliced
- ¼ red onion - sliced
- ½ cup of feta cheese
- ½ cup of pitted Kalamata olives - sliced
- 1 can of artichoke hearts, 14 ounces, drained and cut in half
- 1 large avocado - halved, pitted, and sliced
- 1 can of chickpeas, 14 ounces, drained and rinsed
- 6 cups of Romaine lettuce – chopped

Instructions

For the Greek Chicken Marinated

1. Prepare the meat sauce. Add all of the marinade ingredients (olive oil, garlic, lemon juice, lemon zest, fresh thyme, fresh oregano, fresh rosemary, fresh parsley, salt, and black pepper) to a large, shallow mixing bowl. Mix things up well.
2. Make sure the chicken is tasty. Marinate the chicken for 30 minutes or as long as two hours. Make sure the chicken breasts are well coated with the marinade by mixing them well.

3   Prepare the grill. Set the grill to medium-high heat. Clean the grill grates and use cooking spray or vegetable oil to lightly oil them.

4   Grilling chicken. Put the chicken on the grill as soon as you remove it from the marinade. Discard the remaining marinade. Let the chicken cook for about 5 minutes with the lid on, and then turn the heat down to medium. Give the chicken another 2 minutes to cook, and then use tongs to flip each breast. Grill the chicken for another 5–7 minutes when a digital meat thermometer reads 160°F in the thickest part of the chicken.

5   The chicken needs to rest. Take the chicken breasts off the grill and place them on a clean plate. Wait 5 minutes before you cut through the foil.

For Greek Vinaigrette

1.   Put all of the vinaigrette's ingredients into a medium-sized jar. Cover with a lid that fits well and shake hard until everything is mixed well. Put away or put in the fridge until you are ready to use.

To make the salad

1.   Get vegetables ready and cut them up. While the chicken is cooking, chop the lettuce, artichoke hearts, cucumber, bell pepper, red onion, tomatoes, and olives and put them in a large salad bowl. Mix with a gentle toss.

2.   Assemble. Cut up the grilled chicken breasts and add them to the salad. Top with chickpeas, feta cheese, and sliced avocado. Drizzle with Greek vinaigrette. If you want, you can serve it with fresh dill and parsley on top. Enjoy!

GRILLED CHEEK CHICKEN SALAD

Prep Time: 15 Minutes

Total Times: 15 Minutes

Serving: 1

Ingredients

- 1/2 cup of tortilla strips
- 2 tbsp hot honey (find my recipe here or use store-bought)
- 6 cups of mixed green lettuce
- 3/4 cup of corn
- 1 avocado, sliced
- 1/2 cup of diced peppers
- 3/4 cup of chipotle ranch dressing (find my recipe here or use store-bought)
- 3/4 cup of shredded pepper jack cheese
- 1 cup of sliced chicken strips
- 3/4 cup of sliced tomatoes
- 3/4 cup of black beans, rinsed and drained
- 1/4 cup of diced red onion

Instructions

1. Place the chopped lettuce in a bowl or a plate with a rim.
2. Add tomatoes, corn, black beans, shredded pepper jack cheese, diced peppers, red onion, sliced avocado, and tortilla chips.
3. Before serving, put warm chicken slices on top and drizzle with hot honey and chipotle ranch dressing.

CURRY CHICKEN SALAD WITH GRAPES

Prep Time: 15 Minutes

Cook Time: 25 Minutes

Total Times: 40 Minutes

Serving: 2-4

Ingredients

- 1/4 cup of diced celery and A few cracks of black pepper
- 1 cup of toasted slivered almonds (One 2 ounce packet), *See notes.
- 1/8 tsp kosher or sea salt; more to taste if needed
- 2 cups of chopped or shredded cooked chicken
- 2 TBSP plain Greek yogurt, More if desired.
- 1 tsp curry powder and 2 scallions, thinly sliced
- 1/3 cup of sliced/quartered red grapes; you can use green grapes as well.

Instructions

Chicken

1   If you cook the chicken instead of using already-cooked chicken, preheat the oven to 375o F. About 8 to 9 ounces of boneless, skinless chicken will give you two cups of of raw chicken. You can use breasts or thighs. For this recipe, I used thighs.

2   Keep the chicken on a baking sheet and lightly season with salt and pepper. Brush the chicken with olive oil.

3   Bake the chicken for about 25 minutes, or until the thickest part of the chicken has an internal temperature of 165o F and the juices run clear. When it's done, set it aside to cool down a bit.

Once the chicken has cooled, cut it into small pieces and put them in a large bowl. Set aside.

Chicken Salad

1 You can get the other ingredients ready while the chicken is cooking or cooling. Put the chicken, celery, grapes, almonds that have been toasted, and scallions into the same bowl.

2 Mix in Greek yogurt, curry powder, salt, and pepper. Fold all ingredients with a large spoon or spatula until everything is well-mixed. Taste it and add salt and pepper to your liking. If you want it to be creamier, add more Greek yogurt until you get the right texture. (It's not mayo, after all.)

3 Serve on whole-grain bread as a sandwich or on greens as a salad.

LEMON TARRAGON CHICKEN SALAD

Prep Time: 15 Minutes

Total Times: 15 Minutes

Serving: 2-4

Ingredients

- ½ tsp. salt
- 2 celery stalks diced
- 2 lbs. chicken breast cooked
- 2 tbsp. stone ground mustard
- ¼ cup of fresh tarragon chopped
- ½ cup of mayo
- 3 lemons zested and juiced

- ½ tsp. pepper
- 2 tbsp. fresh parsley chopped
- 4 green onions chopped

Instructions

1. Start by cutting the cooked chicken into pieces that are easy to eat.
2. Add the chicken, mayonnaise, lemon zest and juice, stone-ground mustard, diced celery, and chopped herbs to a large mixing bowl.
3. Stir to coat the chicken all over.
4. Salt and pepper can be added to taste.

MANGO CURRIED CHICKEN SALAD

Prep Time: 10 Minutes

Total Times: 10 Minutes

Serving: 4

Ingredients

- ½ cup of honey mustard
- 2 rib celery chopped
- ½ cup of chopped dried or fresh mango
- ½ cup of mayonnaise or plain Greek yogurt
- Leafy greens
- ½ cup of chopped cashews

- 1 small rotisserie chicken picked (reserve 2 tbsp chicken juices)
- 1 tbsp curry powder
- Optional: 4-6 bagels or croissants

Instructions

1. Shred the rotisserie chicken and put it in a big bowl. Add 1-2 tbsp of the chicken juices if you want.
2. Cut up the mango, cashews, and celery. Add to bowl.
3. Add mayonnaise and honey mustard and mix well.
4. Bagels or croissants can be toasted. To make a sandwich, spread chicken salad on the bottom half of each bagel or croissant, add a layer of leafy greens, and then cover with the other half. Enjoy!

BUFFALO CHICKEN SALAD

Prep Time: 15 Minutes

Total Times: 15 Minutes

Serving: 4

Ingredients

- 1 stick celery chopped
- 2 tbsp mayo
- 1/4 cup of blue cheese dressing
- 2 cups of cooked/rotisserie chicken diced/chopped
- 1 tbsp Frank's Red Hot Original Sauce
- 1-2 tbsp red onion or scallions chopped

- 1 tsp lemon juice
- Salt & pepper to taste
- For serving: 8 slices of bread, lettuce, etc.

Instructions

1. Prep all the ingredients, then add the dressing ingredients to a prep bowl (blue cheese dressing, mayo, Frank's Red Hot, lemon juice) and stir together until smooth.
2. Add in the cooked chicken, celery, and onions. Toss together. Taste and adjust ingredients if needed (you may want to add more hot sauce or blue cheese dressing, for example) and season with salt & pepper as needed. This chicken salad isn't very spicy, as written.
3. Assemble sandwiches/wraps/etc. or enjoy as-is.

CRANBERRY WALNUT CHICKEN SALAD

Prep Time: 15 Minutes

Total Times: 15 Minutes

Serving: 4

Ingredients

For the dressing

- 1 tbsp apple cider vinegar
- 1 tbsp honey
- 1/4 tsp pepper
- 1/2 tsp salt

- 1/4 cup of mayonnaise
- 1/4 cup of plain Greek yogurt
- 1/8 tsp garlic powder

For the chicken salad

- 2 stalks of celery diced
- 1/4 cup of sliced green onion
- 2 cups of diced cooked chicken
- 1/3 cup of chopped walnuts
- 1/3 cup of dried cranberries

Instructions

1. In a small bowl, whisk the Greek yogurt, mayonnaise, vinegar, honey, salt, pepper, and garlic powder until well blended.
2. Add diced chicken, celery, dried cranberries, walnuts, and green onion to a medium bowl. Add dressing and toss gently to combine.
3. If you have time, cover and refrigerate for several hours or overnight.

CALIFORNIA CHICKEN SALAD

Prep Time: 15 Minutes

Total Times: 15 Minutes

Serving: 4

Ingredients

- 1/2 cup of red onion, finely chopped
- 4 cups of rotisserie chicken, chopped
- 1/2 cup of cilantro, finely chopped
- juice of two limes (about 4 tbsp) to taste
- freshly ground black pepper, to taste
- 1-2 large avocados, diced
- 1/2 cup of mayonnaise

Instructions

1. If you are using rotisserie chicken, remove all breast meat. Then shred or chop to your desired size.
2. In a large bowl, add chicken and all the salad ingredients.
3. Mix gently until everything is combined. Add more lime juice and freshly ground black pepper if you like.
4. Serve immediately or chill until you are ready to serve.

THAI GRILLED CHICKEN SALAD

Prep Time: 20 Minutes

Cook Time: 20 Minutes

Marinating Time: 3 hours

Total Times: 15 Minutes

Serving: 4

Ingredients

- 4 tbsp roasted peanuts
- 100g/3 nests rice noodles
- 2 carrots
- 3-4 mint leaves for garnish optional
- 4 green/spring onions
- ½ Long English cucumber
- 4 tbsp Thai red curry paste for the marinade
- 20g/1/2 cup of fresh cilantro/coriander
- ⅓ head red cabbage
- 4 skinless boneless chicken breasts

For the dressing

- 1 tbsp Sriracha sauce or ½ tsp chili flakes
- 1 clove garlic grated or pressed
- 2 tbsp boiling water
- ½ tbsp grated ginger or jarred ginger paste
- 3 tbsp soy sauce
- salt to taste
- 3 tbsp crunchy peanut butter
- 1 ½ limes juice and zest

Instructions

1   Cut each chicken breast in half lengthwise, then pound the thicker part of the chicken breast to flatten and even it out. Spread the red curry paste all over the chicken breasts and let them marinate for 2-3 hours in a refrigerator. Place the chicken breasts on a preheated grill on high heat and grill for 2 minutes on each side, then move to the indirect heat, cover the lid of the grill, and cook for 5-7 minutes until cooked all the way through and the internal temperature reads 165F/74C. Rest for 5 minutes before serving.

2   Make the salad dressing by mixing the peanut butter with boiling water to loosen it a bit, then stir in the soy sauce, grated ginger or ginger paste, sriracha sauce, pressed garlic, and the zest and juice of 1 ½ limes.

3   Prepare the rice noodles according to the package instructions. Slice the red cabbage thinly, then cut the carrots and cucumber in thin long strips. Use a julienne vegetable peeler if you have one. Chop the cilantro and slice the green onions.

4   Drain and rinse the noodles in cold water, then combine them with the vegetables and toss with the peanut dressing reserving 3-4 tbsp of the dressing. Add salt to taste. Serve topped with sliced grilled chicken and chopped peanuts. Drizzle the reserved dressing all over the chicken breasts before serving.

CHINESE CAULIFLOWER SALAD WITH SHREDDED CHICKEN

Prep Time: 20 Minutes

Cook Time: 20 Minutes

Total Times: 40 Minutes

Serving: 4

Ingredients

Salad

- ½ cup of chives, chopped
- 3 tbsp Chinese cooking wine
- 1 Chinese cauliflower
- ½ tbsp avocado oil
- 2 cup of chicken broth
- 4 chicken tenderloin
- ¾ cup of water, divided
- 1 garlic clove
- 1 handful of lettuce, purple coral
- 4 slices ginger

Salad Dressing

- 2 tbsp plum sauce
- 4 tbsp rice wine vinegar
- 1 ½ ginger, grated
- 1 tbsp olive oil

Instructions

Salad

1   In a small saucepan on medium to high heat, bring 2 cups of chicken broth to a boil. Add 3 tbsp of Chinese cooking wine and 4 slices of ginger into the broth. Once it starts to boil, add the chicken tenderloin strips and boil for 10 minutes.
2   Remove the chicken and set aside to cool. Shred the chicken by pulling the flesh apart with your fingers. Set aside.
3   Cut the Chinese cauliflower into small florets.
4   On medium to high heat, add ½ tbsp of avocado oil to a wok. Once that is hot, add 1 chopped garlic clove. Fry for 45 seconds.
5   Add the Chinese cauliflower, followed by ¼ cup of water, into the wok. Stir fry for 2 minutes. Add another ¼ cup of water and stir fry for another 2 minutes. If all the water continues to dry up, add another ¼ cup of and fry for another 2 minutes. Once that is cooked, remove the cooked Chinese cauliflower with a pair of tongs. Do not scoop it out or pour it out, as we don't want the garlic or the sauce for the salad.
6   Cut a handful of purple coral lettuce thinly.
7   Cut the chives about 3 cm in length to yield ½ cup.

Salad Dressing

1   Peel the ginger and grate enough to yield 1 ½ tsp.
2   In a small mixing bowl, add the rice wine vinegar, plum sauce, olive oil, and grated ginger until well combined.

Assembly

1   Put all of the salad's ingredients into a large bowl.
2   Now, pour the dressing all over the salad and mix it together well.
3   Put a big pile of mixed salad on a large plate. Serve right away.

CHICKPEA SALAD

BABY CAULIFLOWER AND SPICED CHICKPEAS WITH BEETROOT TAHINI

Prep Time: 20 Minutes

Cook Time: 25 Minutes

Total Times: 45 Minutes

Serving: 4

Ingredients

Salad

- 1 can chickpeas
- pepper, to taste
- 8 baby cauliflower
- 2 ½ tbsp olive oil
- 2½ tsp paprika
- 1 tsp cumin powder, ground
- 1 tsp cayenne pepper
- salt, to taste
- ½ cup of pistachio kernels

Salad Dressing

- pepper, to taste
- ½ cup of tahini
- 3 beetroot
- 2 garlic cloves
- salt, to taste
- 3 tbsp lemon juice

Instructions

Salad

1. Bring a lot of water to a boil in a large pot. First, put the baby cauliflower in the boiling water and let it boil for 8 minutes. Take it out of the water and put it somewhere to cool down.

2. Once it's at room temperature, baste it with 1 tbsp of olive oil and salt it. Next, place on a baking sheet and bake for 20 minutes at 200 C or 400 F, or until golden brown. Take out and put somewhere to cool.

3. Drain the chickpeas from the can and pat them dry. Mix together 1 tsp olive oil, ground cumin, cayenne pepper, paprika, and salt in a bowl. Add the chickpeas and stir well to coat them.

4. Put the coated chickpeas on a baking sheet and bake them at 200 C for 20 minutes. At 10 minutes, take the sheet pan out and shake it so the vegetables roast evenly. After 20 minutes, take them out and put them somewhere to cool. Chop pistachio kernels into small pieces.

Salad Dressing

1. Bring some water in a small pot to a boil. Take off the beetroot's leaves and stem and put it in the pot.

2. Reduce to a simmer and place the lid on.

3. Simmer for at least 30 minutes until they are tender.

4. Remove from the pot, let it cool and with your fingers remove the skin, which should slide off easily.

5. With a hand blender, puree the beetroot, tahini, garlic cloves, lemon juice, a pinch of salt and pepper.

Assembly

1   Using a big flat platter, smear half the plate with the beetroot tahini.

2   Place the roasted baby cauliflower on the side with no tahini.

3   Place the spiced chickpeas next to the baby cauliflower. The idea is you want to be able to see the vibrant purple of the beetroot.

4   Sprinkle the salad with chopped pistachio kernels all around the plate, including the spaces that have nothing on it. Don't put too much on the beetroot tahini so you can continue to make those colours come through.

5   With ½ tsp of olive oil, make small droplets on the outer rim of the plate.

6   Serve immediately as the chickpeas will start to get soft on the beetroot tahini.

ROASTED CHICKPEA AVOCADO SALAD

Prep Time: 10 Minutes

Cook Time: 30 Minutes

Total Times: 40 Minutes

Serving: 4

Ingredients

For the Tahini Dressing

- 1 tsp garlic powder
- 3 tbsp fresh lime or lemon juice
- 1 tbsp pure maple syrup
- 5 tbsp tahini (75 g)
- 3 tbsp water (or more to adjust consistency)
- 1 tsp sea salt

For the Roasted Chickpeas

- 1 tsp extra virgin olive oil
- 1/2 tsp sea salt
- 19 ounce chickpeas, drained and rinsed (approx. 2.5 cups)
- 1/2 tsp cumin
- 1/2 tsp coriander

For the Kale Salad

- 8 tbsp hemp seeds (2 tbsp per bowl)
- 1/4 tsp olive oil
- 6 cups of finely chopped kale (approx. 1 large handful per salad)
- 2 avocado, peeled, pit removed and sliced (about 1/2 an avocado per bowl)

Instructions

1. Preheat the oven to 350 F.
2. Prepare the chickpeas by draining them and giving them a thorough rinse. Place them on a dish towel, fold it over them and roll them around until they're near completely dry. The drier, the better. If some of the skins come off that's good, you can pick those out. For the crispiest chickpeas, remove all the skins.

3   Place the dried chickpeas on a baking tray and drizzle them with the olive oil, rolling around so they're all coated. Roast for 30-40 minutes until golden brown. When they come out of the oven add the spices and roll around to coat. They will get crispy as they cool.

4   Now, put all the ingredients for the dressing in a bowl and whisk until smooth and creamy.

5   Finely chop the kale and drizzle it with the olive oil. Massage it with your hands for about a minute until it's all dark green and has softened up.

6   Either create 1 large salad by mixing everything together in a serving or mixing bowl or my preferred method, divide the kale between 4 servings or bowls, top with equal amounts of the sliced avocado, chickpea and hemp seeds and drizzle each with the dressing until you've used it all up.

———— ◆ ————

PICKLED BEET SALAD WITH CHICKPEA MASH

Prep Time: 15 Minutes

Cook Time: 30 Minutes

Pickling Time: 30 Minutes

Total Times: 1 Hour 15 Minutes

Serving: 4

Ingredients

- ½ cup of water
- ¼ cup of Greek yogurt
- ¼ red onion
- 2 garlic clove
- 3 sprigs lemon thyme
- 1 tsp lemon juice
- 2 beets, medium
- ⅓ cup of sugar, white
- ½ cup of red wine vinegar
- 1 can chickpeas, 400 g
- 1 tsp lemon zest salt, to taste
- pepper, to taste
- 1 tbsp olive oil, extra virgin

Instructions

Salad

1. Cover the beets with cold water in a small saucepan. Bring the pot to a boil, then cook the beets for about 30 minutes, or until they are soft. Let the water run out and let it cool down. Peel the beets and cut them into squares that are 1 cm on a side.
2. Peel a red onion and cut it into thin half-moons.
3. Wash a few lemon thyme sprigs.
4. Mix red wine vinegar, water, white sugar, salt, and pepper in a small saucepan. On low heat, stir it until there is no more sugar.
5. In a bowl, combine the beets, thyme, red onion, and red wine vinegar pickling liquid. Put it in a plastic bag and put it in the refrigerator to pickle. Leave for at least 30 minutes, but preferably overnight.

6   Drain and rinse the canned chickpeas before putting them in a food processor. To taste, add 3 tbsp of yogurt, 2 garlic cloves, lemon juice, lemon zest, salt, and pepper. Blitz until the texture is semi-coarse.

7   Shake the rocket leaves dry after washing them.

Assembly

1   Put a scoop of chickpea mash on a large plate and spread it out in a circle.

2   On top of the chickpea mash, put 1 tbsp of Greek yogurt.

3   Next, put rocket leaves in layers.

4   Last, put pickled beet salad on top.

5   To finish, sprinkle on some cracked black pepper and a little extra virgin olive oil.

6   Serve.

MEDITERRANEAN CHICKPEA SALAD

Prep Time: 15 Minutes

Total Times: 15 Minutes

Serving: 4

Ingredients

- 1/4 cup of feta cheese
- 1 red bell pepper, diced
- 1 cup of Tuscan kale, stems removed & chopped
- 2 cups of cherry tomatoes, halved

- 1 cup of English cucumber, sliced
- 1/2 red onion, thinly sliced
- 14 ounce chickpeas, drained and rinsed
- 1/3 cup of pitted kalamata olives

Dressing

- 1 1/2 tsp fresh parsley, chopped (or 1 tsp dried)
- 1/2 tsp (each) salt & black pepper
- 1 tsp fresh oregano (or 1/2 tsp dried)
- 1-2 tsp maple syrup (or honey)
- 2 Tbsp lemon juice
- 1 garlic clove, minced (or 1/2 tsp garlic powder)
- 1/4 cup of olive oil
- 2 Tbsp red wine vinegar

Instructions

1. Mix the ingredients for the dressing with a whisk. All of the ingredients for the vinaigrette should be put in a liquid measuring cup or small bowl and whisked together. Set it aside.

2. Assemble salad: In a large salad bowl, arrange chopped veggies, chickpeas, olives, feta cheese, and drizzle with dressing. Toss until salad ingredients are evenly coated in the vinaigrette. Taste, adjust flavor with additional salt & black pepper if needed, and then serve!

CHICKPEA TUNA SALAD

Prep Time: 15 Minutes

Total Times: 15 Minutes

Serving: 4

Ingredients

- 1/4 red onion (minced)
- 1/2 cup of Kalamata olives (pitted and minced)
- 1/2 cucumber (seeded and diced)
- 15-ounce of chickpeas (rinsed and drained)
- 2 4.6 ounce cans tuna (packed in oil or water, drained)
- 1 red bell pepper (diced)
- ¼ cup of minced fresh parsley

Dressing

- 1 tsp Dijon mustard
- 1 tsp dried oregano
- 1/2 tsp freshly ground black pepper
- 1/4 cup of lemon juice
- 2 cloves garlic (grated or finely minced)
- 1 tsp kosher salt
- 1/2 cup of extra virgin olive oil

Instructions

1 First, drain the tuna and flake it into a salad bowl.

2 Add the chickpeas, cucumber, red pepper, onion, Kalamata olives, and parsley. Toss gently.

3   Whisk together the dressing ingredients and add them to the
    salad bowl. Toss everything together to coat.

4   Depending on your taste, add more salt and pepper. Enjoy!

GOLDEN CHICKEN AND CHICKPEA SALAD

Prep Time: 25 Minutes

Cook Time: 35 Minutes

Total Times: 1 Hour

Serving: 4 Cups

Ingredients

- 15 ounce chickpeas (drained)
- 1 tbsp minced garlic
- 1 tbsp ground cumin
- 2 cups of broccoli (cut into bite-sized pieces)
- 1 tbsp cilantro
- 2 cups of almond milk
- 1 lb chicken breast (boneless, skinless)
- 3 tbsp red wine vinegar
- 1 tbsp ground turmeric
- 1 tbsp curry powder
- 1/4 cup of olive oil
- 3 ounce spinach and arugula
- 1 1/2 tsp salt

Instructions

1. Whisk the milk, curry powder, turmeric, garlic, and 1 tsp salt in a large saucepan over medium heat until it begins to simmer, stirring occasionally.
2. Add the chicken and chickpeas

3   Cook, covered, occasionally turning, until the chicken is cooked through to an internal temperature of 165F, about 20 minutes

4   Transfer the chicken and chickpeas to a plate, then pour the packing liquid through a mesh strainer into a mixing bowl

5   Transfer 1/2 cup of the liquid to a mini food processor or blender (such as the Magic Bullet blender)

6   Add the olive oil, red wine vinegar, and remaining 1/2 tsp salt and process until smooth

7   Shred the chicken and add the chicken, chickpeas, spinach and arugula, broccoli, and cilantro to a large bowl

8   Drizzle with the dressing and serve immediately

CHICKPEA CURRY SALAD WITH APPLES AND RAISINS

Prep Time: 10 Minutes

Total Times: 10 Minutes

Serving: 6

Ingredients

- ¼ cup of raisins
- 1 gala apple finely diced
- 2 stalks of celery finely diced
- 15 ounce can of chickpeas
- ½ cup of red onion finely diced

Vegan Curry Dressing

- 1 clove garlic finely minced
- ¼ tsp salt
- ¼ tsp pepper
- 1 tsp yellow curry powder
- ½ cup of dairy-free plain coconut yogurt

Instructions

1. In a bowl, whisk together the coconut milk yogurt, minced garlic, curry powder, salt, and pepper. Set aside.
2. Finely dice the apple, two stalks of celery, and red onion. Set aside.
3. If using canned chickpeas, drain and rinse one 15-ounce can.
4. In a large bowl, add the chickpeas, celery, onion, diced apple, and raisins. Pour the dressing overtop. Mix well with a spatula. Serve cold!

CHICKPEA SALAD WITH FETA

Prep Time: 10 Minutes

Total Times: 10 Minutes

Serving: 4

Ingredients

Salad

- ⅓ cup of parsley, chopped
- 1 red pepper, small
- 1 can chickpeas, 400g/14 ounce
- 200 g cherry tomatoes
- 1 can corn kernels, 400g/14 ounce
- 100 g Greek feta
- 1 cucumber, Lebanese

Salad Dressing

- 2 tbsp lemon juice
- 1 garlic clove, crushed
- 3 tbsp olive oil, extra virgin
- pepper,salt to taste

Instructions

Salad

1   Open and drain canned chickpeas. Give chickpeas a rinse under water before using.
2   Open and drain canned corn.
3   Chop cucumber into small pieces.

4   Cut cherry tomatoes into halves.

5   Slice and cut bell peppers into bite-size pieces.

6   Roughly chop parsley.

Salad Dressing

1   In a mason jar, add extra virgin olive oil, lemon juice, garlic, salt
     and pepper.

2   Shake until well combined.

Assembly

1   In a large bowl, add all the salad ingredients except for feta.

2   Pour dressing on top and toss to combine.

3   Crumb feta on top of the salad and gently toss it through.

4   Serve.

CHICKPEA TOMATO SALAD WITH CREAMY YOGURT DRESSING

Prep Time: 10 Minutes

Cook Time: 40 Minutes

Total Times: 50 Minutes

Serving: 6

Ingredients

For the Roasted Chickpeas

- 1 tsp garlic powder

- Zest from 1 lemon

- 2 (15-ounce) cans of chickpeas

- 1 tsp salt

- 1 tsp freshly ground black pepper

- 2 tbsp olive oil

- ½ tsp smoked paprika

For the Creamy Yogurt Dressing

- ½ cup of fresh parsley - finely chopped
- ¼ tsp garlic powder
- 3 green onions - finely chopped
- salt + pepper - to taste
- ¼ cup of fresh dill - finely chopped juice from 1/2 a lemon
- 2 cups of Plain yogurt
- 5 cloves garlic - minced

For the Salad

- 1 cup of pepperoncini - roughly chopped
- 4 large tomatoes - chopped into large chunks
- ½ small red onion - thinly sliced
- 2 tbsp fresh parsley - chopped
- 1 serrano or jalapeño pepper - diced
- 1 large English Cucumber - diced
- 2 red bell peppers

Instructions

For the Chickpeas

1   Set the oven to 375°F and put parchment paper on a large baking sheet with a rim. Set aside.

2   While the oven heats up, drain and rinse the chickpeas from two cans. Move the chickpeas to a clean dish towel or a couple of paper towels stacked together. Rub the chickpeas gently with another dry paper towel or dish towel. The skins will begin to come off, which is fine.

3   Now, place the chickpeas in a bowl and add the olive oil, garlic powder, paprika, salt, and pepper. Toss them gently. Place the chickpeas in a single layer on the prepared baking sheet and bake for 35 to 40 minutes. Save the mixing bowl with any extra oil or seasoning.

4   Next, take the chickpeas out of the oven and let them cool for 2 minutes. Then, put them in a mixing bowl and carefully toss them with the lemon zest and any extra olive oil. (I

5   had approximately 1 tsp remaining).

6   Put the chickpeas back on the baking sheet in one layer and let them cool completely.

For the dressing made with creamy yogurt

1   Put everything in a medium bowl and stir well to mix. Add more salt and pepper to suit your taste.

2   For the Roasted Red Bell Peppers (optional)

3   Get the oven ready to broil. Now, line a baking sheet with foil and lightly spray it with cooking spray that won't stick.

4   Roast bell peppers for 10 to 15 minutes, turning them every 5 minutes to make sure both sides get the same amount of cooking time. Take peppers out of the oven when they are charred and soft on both sides. Wrap the peppers carefully in foil (they will be hot), and let them steam for 5 minutes.

5 Unwrap the bell peppers and let them cool for a few minutes before taking off the stem, scooping out the seeds, and cutting the peppers into chunks.

Assemble the Salad

1 In a large salad bowl, add the roasted bell peppers, tomatoes, cucumber, red onion, pepperoncini, serrano pepper, and fresh parsley.

2 Gently toss to combine. Just before serving, top with the crispy chickpeas and drizzle with the desired amount of homemade creamy yogurt dressing

INDIAN CHICKPEA SALAD

Prep Time: 15 Minutes

Total Times: 15 Minutes

Serving: 4

Ingredients

- 1 cup of fresh pomegranate seeds
- 1 small red onion - thinly chopped
- 1/2 mixed nuts (as per your choice)
- 1 Large tomato - thinly chopped
- 2 cups of cooked chickpeas
- 1 large cucumber - thinly chopped
- 1/4 cup of fresh cilantro - thinly chopped
- Juice of 2 large lemon

- Optional: 4 tbsp feta cheese

Spices

- 1/2 tsp Red Chili powder
- 1 tsp Salt (add more as per choice)
- 1 tbsp Chat masala
-

Instructions

1 First, mix all the ingredients in a bowl and all the spices.
2 Mix everything and taste test for seasoning (salt/pepper)
3 Serve immediately or store in an air-tight box in the fridge for 6-7 hrs.

GARBANZO EGG SALAD

Prep Time: 6 Minutes

Total Times: 6 Minutes

Serving: 12

Ingredients

Dressing

- 1 tsp dried crushed red pepper
- 1 tsp paprika
- 1/3 cup of extra virgin olive oil
- 1 tsp Tajin
- 1 orange, zest and juice

- 1 tbsp hot sauce
- 1 lime, zest and juice and 1 garlic clove, minced
- T2 sp spicy brown mustard

Egg Salad

- 1/2 cup of chopped fresh mint leaves
- 2 (16-ounce) cans of chickpeas, rinsed and drained
- Pepitas for garnish
- 1/2 cup of thinly sliced or shredded red cabbage
- 2 stalks celery, chopped and 1 large English cucumber, diced
- 5 Nellie's Free Range Eggs, hard-boiled, peeled, and sliced
- 1 serrano pepper, diced
- ¼ chopped red onions
- 1/2 cup of chopped cilantro leaves

Instructions

1. In a mason jar, combine the dressing ingredients, cover, shake, and set aside.
2. In a mixing bowl, add all the salad ingredients except the eggs and pepitas.
3. Pour dressing over salad and combine. Add the sliced eggs and pepitas and gently toss. Taste and adjust with salt or Tajin if needed.
4. Cover and refrigerate until ready to serve. The longer this salad marinates, the better the flavor.
5. In a container with a tight lid, salad will keep well in the fridge for 2 to 3 days.

GREEK CUCUMBER SALAD

Prep Time: 10 Minutes

Total Times: 10 Minutes

Serving: 8

Ingredients

- ¼ cup of kalamata olives
- ½ tsp. salt
- ½ pint cherry tomatoes cut in half
- 1 cup of baby spinach finely chopped
- ¼ cup of extra virgin olive oil
- 1 can garbanzo beans (chickpeas), drained and rinsed
- 1 tbsp fresh parsley, roughly chopped
- 2 tbsp. crumbled feta cheese
- ½ small red onion, thinly sliced
- ½ cucumber partially peeled and cut into ½ inch chunks
- 2 tbsp. Red wine vinegar

Instructions

1. In a medium bowl, add spinach, cucumber, tomatoes, olives, parsley, red onions, drained chickpeas, and feta.
2. Stir to combine.
3. Pour red wine vinegar and olive oil over the top and season with salt.

CHICKPEA BROCCOLI SALAD

Prep Time: 25 Minutes

Cook Time: 5 Minutes

Total Times: 30 Minutes

Serving: 4

Ingredients

- ¼ cup of Kalamata olives pitted and sliced
- 400 ml chickpeas drained and rinsed (approximately 1 2/3 cups)
- 4 cups of raw broccoli florets
- ¼ cup of fresh parsley, washed, dried chopped
- ¼ cup of red onion finely chopped
- ¼ cup of Feta cheese crumbled

Olive oil Lemon Vinaigrette

- ¼ tsp black pepper, freshly ground
- ½ tsp sea salt
- ¼ cup of extra-virgin olive oil
- 1 garlic clove, minced small
- 3 tbsp lemon juice freshly squeezed

Instructions

1   Rinse broccoli florets and steam for 5 to 7 minutes, or until just tender. Remove broccoli from the steamer and set aside to let cool.

2   Meanwhile, prepare the olive oil and lemon vinaigrette. Add all of the vinaigrette ingredients to a jar, shake well and set aside until ready to use.

3   In a large bowl, combine steamed broccoli florets, chickpeas, red onion, olives, parsley and half of the Feta cheese. Add 3/4 of the dressing, toss well and taste. If needed, add the remaining dressing. Top salad with remaining crumbled Feta cheese.

4   Serve right away or put in the refrigerator until you're ready to eat.

CARROT, CHICKPEA AND RAISIN SALAD

Prep Time: 15-20 Minutes

Freeze Time: 30 Minutes

Total Times: 45-50 Minutes

Serving: 8

Ingredients

Citrus Vinaigrette

- ¾ tsp coarse salt
- Zest and juice of 1 small orange
- 1 tbsp white wine or champagne vinegar
- 1 ½ tbsp honey
- ¼ tsp freshly ground black pepper
- 3 tbsp olive oil
- Zest and juice of 1 small lemon

- 1-inch piece of ginger, finely grated

Salad

- ½ cup of fresh cilantro leaves, chopped
- 1 cup of raisins
- ¼ cup of sliced almonds
- 1 pound carrots, peeled and shredded (about 4-5 cups)
- 15-ounce can of chickpeas, rinsed and drained
- Optional: ¼ cup of crumbled feta

Instructions

1. Place the dressing ingredients in a jar fitted with a lid and shake until well combined.
2. Place the carrots, chickpeas, raisins, cilantro and almonds in a bowl. Add the dressing and toss to combine. Refrigerate for at least 30 minutes.
3. Top with feta right before serving, if desired.

ROASTED BUTTERNUT SQUASH SALAD

Prep Time: 20 Minutes

Cook Time: 40 Minutes

Total Times: 60 Minutes

Serving: 8

Ingredients

Honey Apple Vinaigrette Dressing

- 1 tbsp honey and 1/4 tsp salt
- 2 tbsp apple cider vinegar
- 1/8 tsp black pepper
- 1 tsp Dijon mustard
- 2 tbsp extra-virgin olive oil

Salad

- 1/8 tsp black pepper
- 1 medium sweet onion diced
- 1 tsp salt divided
- 5 cups of chopped fresh kale and 2 tbsp of olive oil
- 1 1/2 pounds of butternut squash peeled, de-seeded, and cubed into 1/2-inch pieces
- 1 1/2 cups of water and 1 cup of pearl couscous
- 15.5-ounce can of chickpeas rinsed and drained

Instructions

1. Mix the dressing's ingredients together in a bowl with a whisk, then set it aside.

2. Turn the oven on to 425F. On the baking sheet, mix the cubed squash, olive oil, 3/4 tsp of salt, and black pepper. Then, spread the squash out in a single layer. Roast the squash, turning it once halfway through, until it is soft and golden in spots, about 20 to 30 minutes. Cool.

3. In the meantime, bring a medium saucepan of water to a boil. The water should be boiling when you add the pearl couscous and the last 1/4 tsp of salt. Bring to a boil again, then turn the heat down to a simmer. Cover the pot and let it cook for about

20 minutes or until all the water is gone. Put out the fire and let it cool down.

4   Mix the butternut squash, pearl couscous, onion, kale, chickpeas, and salad dressing together in a large bowl. And serve.

GREEK SALAD

HORIATIKI (GREEK VULLAGE SALAD)

Prep Time: 15 Minutes

Total Times: 15 Minutes

Serving: 6

Ingredients

- 1 small cucumber, halved lengthwise and cut in 1/2-inch slices
- 2 tbsp red wine vinegar
- ½ cup of red onion, thinly sliced
- ½ tsp dried oregano, crushed
- ⅓ cup of kalamata olives, pitted and halved
- 1 4 ounce triangle high-quality sheep's milk feta cheese
- 1 medium green bell pepper, cut in bite-sized pieces
- 3 medium Roma tomatoes (9 ounce) or 6 ounce grape tomatoes
- 2 tbsp extra-virgin olive oil
- ½ tsp coarse sea salt
- Optional: 1 tbsp capers

Instructions

1   Cut the tomatoes into bite-sized pieces (or in half if you are using grape tomatoes) over a serving bowl to catch any juices.
2   Add to the bowl with the cucumber, green bell pepper, red onion, and kalamata olives. Throw around to mix.
3   Add feta cheese to the top. Sprinkle the salad and cheese with olive oil and red wine vinegar.
4   You can sprinkle it with oregano, salt, and capers.

Main Dish

1   Add 4 ounces of cooked chicken breast, salmon or shrimp to salad to make it a complete meal.

GREEK INSPIRED QUINOA SALAD WITH LEMON FETA DRESSING

Prep Time: 30 Minutes

Cook Time: 15 Minutes

Total Times: 45 Minutes

Serving: 4

Ingredients

- 1 ¼ cup of sliced miniature red, yellow, and/or orange bell peppers
- ¼ cup of sliced red onion
- ½ cup of pitted Kalamata olives
- ¼ cup of olive oil
- 2 cup of chopped baby spinach
- 1 large lemon (2 tsp. zest, 1/4 cup of juice)
- 1 tsp dried oregano, crushed
- 1 15 ounce of can chickpeas, rinsed and drained
- ⅓ cup of crumbled feta cheese
- 1 ¼ cup of chopped cucumber
- 1 ½ cup of pita chips
- ¾ cup of quinoa, rinsed and drained

Instructions

2   Bring 1 1/2 cups of water and the quinoa to a boil in a medium-sized saucepan, then reduce the heat.

3   Now cover and let simmer for 15 minutes, or until all the water is absorbed. Spread the quinoa out to cool on a large baking sheet.

4   Meantime, make dressing by whisking together the lemon zest and juice, feta, olive oil, oregano, and 1 tsp. salt in a small bowl.

5   Mix the cooled quinoa with half of the dressing in a medium bowl. Spread spinach out on a serving dish. Pour the quinoa mix on top.

6   Put chickpeas, bell peppers, cucumber, and olives on a platter. Pour the rest of the dressing over everything and top with red onion.

7   Add pita chips to the top. If you want, you can drizzle with more olive oil.

KALE FALAFEL SALAD WITH TOASTED PINE NUTS

Prep Time: 20 Minutes

Cook Time: 20 Minutes

Total Times: 40 Minutes

Serving: 4

Ingredients

- 1 ¼ cup of chopped English cucumber
- ¼ cup of fresh flat-leaf parsley
- 1 10 ounce container hummus
- 2 cup of fresh baby spinach
- 2 tbsp of chopped fresh oregano
- 1 12 ounce pkg. of frozen cooked falafel
- 1 cup of grape tomatoes, halved
- 2 tbsp red wine vinegar
- ½ cup of thinly sliced red onion
- 3 ounce of feta cheese, sliced or 1/3 cup of crumbled feta cheese
- 1 6 ounce bunch curly kale, stems removed, and leaves torn
- ¼ cup of pine nuts, toasted

Instructions

1. In a small mixing bowl, combine and mix vinegar, 1 tsp of water, a pinch of salt, and the onion.
2. Cover and let stand for 20 to 30 minutes at room temperature. Drain the onion and save the pickling liquid.
3. In a large bowl, mix the pickling liquid you saved, 2 tbsp of olive oil, and a pinch of salt with the kale.
4. About 3 minutes, or until the kale is bright green and soft, rub it with your hands.
5. Spread hummus out on a serving dish. Place the kale, spinach, cucumber, tomatoes, feta cheese, pine nuts, pickled onion, parsley, and oregano on top.
6. Add 1/4 tsp of ground black pepper.
7. Falafel goes on top. You can add more olive oil and red wine vinegar if you want.

GREEK ISLES SUPPER SALAD

Prep Time: 35 Minutes

Total Times: 35 Minutes

Serving: 4

Ingredients

- ⅓ cup of Essential Everyday Vinaigrette or desired bottled vinaigrette salad dressing
- 1 13.75 ounce can artichoke hearts, drained, rinsed, and quartered
- 2 cup of grape tomatoes, halved
- 2 ounce feta cheese, crumbled
- 8 ounce roasted chicken meat, coarsely shredded*
- 6 ounce small whole grain pasta, such as bow tie or rotini
- ¼ cup of pitted green and/or Kalamata olives, coarsely chopped
- 4 cup of broccoli florets

Essential Everyday Vinaigrette

- 1 clove garlic, minced
- ⅛ tsp salt
- dash ground black pepper
- 1 tbsp Dijon-style mustard
- 1 tsp honey
- 6 tbsp olive oil
- ¼ cup of red wine vinegar

Instructions

1. Follow the directions on the package to cook the pasta, and add the broccoli during the last two minutes of cooking.
2. Drain well. Put into a very large bowl. Tomatoes, artichokes, and olives are good to add. Mix in the Essential Everyday Vinaigrette gently.
3. Divide pasta mixture among four dinner plates. Chicken and feta cheese go on top.
4. Essential Everyday Vinaigrette
5. Mix together olive oil, vinegar, Dijon-style mustard, garlic, honey, salt, and black pepper in a jar with a screw-on lid. Cover and give a good shake.
6. Use right away, or put it in the fridge for up to 5 days. Let it sit out for 30 minutes at room temperature before you use it. Makes about 2/3 cup.

GREEK QUINOA AND AVOCADO SALAD

Prep Time: 15 Minutes

Cook Time: 15 Minutes

Total Times: 30 Minutes

Serving: 4

Ingredients

- ⅓ cup of finely chopped red onion (1 small)
- ½ cup of shredded fresh spinach

- Spinach leaves
- 2 roma tomatoes, seeded and finely chopped
- ½ cup of uncooked quinoa, rinsed and drained*
- ½ tsp salt
- 2 ripe avocados, halved, seeded, peeled, and sliced**
- 2 tbsp lemon juice
- ⅓ cup of crumbled feta cheese
- 2 tbsp olive oil
- 1 cup of water

Instructions

1. Mix quinoa and water in a 1-1/2-quart saucepan. Bring mixture to a boil, then reduce the heat. Now cover the pot and let simmer for approximately 15 minutes or until all the liquid is absorbed.
2. Transfer quinoa to a medium bowl. Stir to mix in the tomato, spinach, and onion. Mix the lemon juice, oil, and salt in a small bowl with a whisk. Add to the quinoa and stir to coat.
3. Put spinach leaves on 4 plates of salad. Put slices of avocado on spinach leaves. Spoon quinoa mixture over avocado slices. Add some feta cheese on top. Serves 4 as a main dish.

GREEK OREGANO CHICKEN WITH SPINACH, ORZO AND GRAPE TOMATOES

Prep Time: 20 Minutes

Cook Time: 4 Hours

Total Times: 4 Hours 20 Minutes

Ingredients

- Snipped fresh oregano
- 2 cup of grape tomatoes
- 2 tbsp lemon juice
- 1 tsp dried oregano, crushed
- ⅛ tsp ground black pepper
- 3 cloves garlic, minced and ¼ tsp salt
- 4 8 ounce of skinless, boneless chicken breast halves
- 1 ½ cup of cooked orzo pasta (rosamarina)
- 1 tsp dried basil, crushed
- 1 tsp finely shredded lemon peel
- 1 tbsp grated Parmesan cheese
- 1 tsp dried parsley, crushed
- 1 tbsp olive oil
- 1 14.5 ounce can reduced-sodium chicken broth
- 1 10 ounce of package frozen chopped spinach, thawed and squeezed dry

Instructions

1. Mix dried oregano, basil, parsley, salt, and pepper in a small bowl. Spread the mixture evenly over the chicken, and use your fingers to work it in.
2. In a large skillet, cook the chicken for about 6 minutes over medium-high heat in hot oil, turning it once. Take off the heat.
3. Mix chicken, broth, and garlic in a slow cooker that holds 3 1/2 or 4 quarts.
4. Add spinach and then put tomatoes on top. Cover and cook for 4 hours on low heat or for 2 hours on high heat.

5   Take the chicken out of the pot. Cover it and keep it warm. Using a slotted spoon, move

6   the spinach and tomatoes to a large bowl. Discard the liquid.

7   Mix spinach with cooked pasta, lemon peel, and lemon juice. Serve the pasta and chicken together. Add cheese and fresh oregano to the top.

PULLED PORK GREEK SALAD

Prep Time: 20 Minutes

Total Times: 20 Minutes

Serving: 4

Ingredients

- 1/4 cup of Italian dressing (purchased or homemade, divided)
- 1/2 pound cooked pulled pork
- 1/2 red onion (cut into 1/4-inch dice)
- 1/2 cup of feta cheese (crumbled)
- 10 cups of romaine lettuce (chopped, about 1 large head)
- 1/2 cup of kalamata olives (halved, pitted)
- small tomatoes (cut into wedges)
- 1/2 cucumber (halved lengthwise and sliced)

Instructions

1   Toss the lettuce with about half of the dressing in a large bowl.

2   Place the salad on plates or a platter and arrange the pork, tomatoes, cucumbers, onions, feta, and olives on top.

3   Drizzle the remaining dressing over the salad and serve.

GREEK TORTELLINI SALAD

Prep Time: 30 Minutes

Total Times: 30 Minutes

Serving: 8

Ingredients

salt

- 1/2 cup of grape tomatoes (halved)
- 3/4 cup of crumbled feta cheese
- 1/2 cup of red onions (diced)
- 20 ounce cheese tortellini (refrigerated)
- 1/4 cup of virgin olive oil
- 1 cucumber (large, chopped)
- 1 clove minced garlic
- 1/2 tsp. oregano (died)
- 3 Tbsp. red wine vinegar
- 1 cup of kalamata olives

Instructions

1. Add salt and pepper to the olive oil, vinegar, garlic, oregano, and garlic. Set aside for dressing.
2. Follow the directions for cooking tortellini. Drain. Use cold water to rinse.
3. Mix the tortellini, cucumber, tomatoes, olives, onion, feta, and dressing in a large bowl. Mix well by tossing.
4. Use cold food.

GRILLED HALLOUMI AND WATERMELON SALAD

Prep Time: 18 Minutes

Total Times: 18 Minutes

Serving: 4

Ingredients

- 6 ounce halloumi (sliced)
- 2 Tbsp. pumpkin seeds
- 1 seedless watermelon (small, cut into quarters)
- 1/2 lime
- 2 Tbsp. fresh mint (chopped)
- 1 pinch cayenne
- 1 Tbsp. honey
- 1/4 cup of grapeseed oil

Instructions

1. Put the grill attachment for the Smart Oven+ in the oven. Choose GRILL Mode and turn the Grill up to High heat.
2. In a small bowl, mix together oil, honey, lime juice, cayenne, and chopped mint. Set dressing aside.
3. Slice halloumi into ¼-inch slices. Place on the grill and cook for 3–4 minutes on each side.
4. Take the meat off the grill and put it on a platter with the watermelon. Sprinkle with pumpkin seeds and drizzle with dressing. Serve right away.

GRILLED GREEK PANZANELLA SALAD

Prep Time: 25 Minutes

Total Times: 25 Minutes

Serving: 6

Ingredients

- 1 English cucumber (seeded and cut into 1-inch chunks)
- 6 Roma tomatoes (seeded and cut into 1-inch chunks)
- 1 Tbsp. chopped fresh mint
- 6 cups of sourdough bread (cubed)
- 2 tsp. minced fresh garlic
- 6 Tbsp. Crisco Pure Vegetable Oil
- 2 Tbsp. fresh lemon juice
- 1/4 cup of crumbled feta cheese

Instructions

1. WHISK together 4 tbsp of oil, lemon juice, and garlic until smooth.
2. HEAT the grill to medium-high. Coat the bread with the two tbsp of oil that are left in a large bowl.
3. Turn the meat often for 4 to 5 minutes, until all sides are lightly charred.
4. Tomatoes, cucumbers, bread, and mint are mixed together in a large bowl. Mix with the sauce. Add salt and pepper to taste. Add cheese on top.

GREEK STYLE CORN SALAD

Prep Time: 15 Minutes

Marinate Time: 1 Hours

Total Times: 1 Hours 15 Minutes

Serving: 2

Ingredients

- pasta (cooked al dente)
- 3 Tbsp. olive oil
- salt and ground black pepper
- 15 black olives (cut into halves)
- 1/2 tsp. oregano (ground)
- 1 Tbsp. Dijon mustard
- 1/2 onion (cut into half moons)
- 2 cups of corn kernels
- 4 Tbsp. balsamic vinegar
- feta cheese
- 1 pinch dill (ground)

Instructions

1. Cook the kernels of corn until they are soft. Drain the water and let it cool.
2. Mix the vinegar, mustard, olive oil, dill, oregano, salt, and pepper together in a bowl with a whisk. Set aside.
3. In a salad bowl, mix the corn, olives, and onion together. Pour the vinaigrette over the vegetables and let them sit for 1 hour.
4. Finally, sprinkle the feta cheese on top of the pasta and salad.

GREEK SQUASH RIBBON SALAD

Prep Time: 30 Minutes

Total Times: 30 Minutes

Serving: 6

Ingredients

- 1 tsp. McCormick Garlic Powder
- 1/2 tsp. McCormick Basil Leaves
- 1/4 cup of red onion (thinly sliced)
- 1/4 cup of fresh lemon juice
- 1 large zucchini
- 1/3 cup of crumbled feta cheese
- 1/2 tsp. McCormick Oregano Leaves
- 1 yellow squash (large)
- 1/2 tsp. salt
- 2 Tbsp. pitted kalamata olives (quartered)
- 1/2 tsp. coarse ground black pepper (McCormick®)
- 1/3 cup of olive oil
- 1/4 cup of white wine vinegar
- 1/2 tsp. mint (McCormick Gourmet™ Organic)
- 1 cup of cherry tomatoes (halved)

Instructions

1   For the Vinaigrette, In a small bowl, use a wire whisk to mix together the oil, lemon juice, vinegar, and spices. Stir in feta cheese. Set aside.

2   For the Salad, trim squash ends. Use vegetable peeler or mandoline to cut the apple into ribbons. Throw away the outside ribbons and the core.

3   To serve, Put strips of squash on each salad plate. Add tomato, onion, and olives on top.

4   Serve with a side of vinaigrette.

GREEK STYLE COLD NOODLE SALAD

Prep Time: 20 Minutes

Total Times: 20 Minutes

Serving: 4

Ingredients

- 1 tsp. McCormick Oregano Leaves
- 1/4 cup of fresh parsley leaves
- 2 Tbsp. olive oil
- 1/2 cup of grape tomatoes (halved)
- 8 ounce udon noodles vinaigrette (Katsu and Oregano)
- 1 Tbsp. red wine vinegar
- 1/4 cup of red bell pepper (thinly sliced)
- 1/4 cup of sliced black olives

Salad (Noodle)

- 1/3 cup of katsu sauce
- 1/4 cup of cucumber (thinly sliced English, seedless, half-moon slices)
- 1/4 cup of pepperoncini (sliced)
- 1/4 cup of crumbled feta cheese
- 1/2 cup of red onion (thinly sliced)

Instructions

1. Mix all of the ingredients for the Katsu and Oregano Vinaigrette in a medium bowl with a wire whisk until they are well blended. Set aside.

2. For the Noodle Salad, cook the udon noodles according to the package's directions. Rinse under cold water. Drain well.

3. Put pasta in a big bowl. Add the vinaigrette and rest of the ingredients, except for the feta cheese, and mix well. Cover.

4. Keep cold for at least an hour. Before you serve it, sprinkle it with feta cheese.

GREEK VEGETABLE SALAD WITH HERB VINAIGRETTE

Prep Time: 15 Minutes

Total Times: 15 Minutes

Serving: 4

Ingredients

- 1/2 cup of olive oil
- 3 cups of cucumbers (seeded and diced, 3/4-inch dice) vinaigrette (Herb)
- 1/4 cup of white wine vinegar
- 1/4 cup of crumbled feta cheese
- 1/2 tsp. McCormick Garlic Powder
- 1 tsp. McCormick Rosemary Leaves
- vegetable salad (Greek)

- 1/2 cup of red onion (thinly sliced)
- 1/2 tsp. McCormick Oregano Leaves
- 1 tsp. McCormick Thyme Leaves
- 3 cups of diced tomatoes (seeded and, 3/4-inch dice)

Instructions

1. For the Herb Vinaigrette, combine and whisk all of ingredients together in a large bowl with a wire whisk until they are well mixed.
2. Add the cucumber, tomatoes, and onion, and toss well to mix. Cover.
3. Place the mixture in the refrigerator for at least an hour or until you are ready to serve. Sprinkle with feta cheese right before serving.

SUMMER CAPRESE SALAD

Prep Time: 15 Minutes

Total Times: 15 Minutes

Serving: 6

Ingredients

- 1 small seedless cucumber, sliced and cut in half
- Kosher salt and freshly ground black pepper
- 3 large tomatoes, sliced
- 1/3 cup of fresh basil leaves
- 2 large peaches, sliced
- 1/2 cup of grape or cherry tomatoes, cut in half

- 1/4 cup of red onion slices
- Balsamic glaze, for drizzling
- 1 pound fresh mozzarella, sliced

152

Instructions

1 Put tomatoes, fresh mozzarella, peaches, cucumbers, grape tomatoes, red onion, and basil leaves on a large platter.
2 Salt and black pepper can be added to taste. Use balsamic glaze to finish. Serve right away.

QUINOA SALAD

QUINOA TABBOULEH SALAD

Prep Time: 20 Mins

Cook Time: 15 Mins

Total Time: 35 Mins

Serving: 6

Ingredients

- 1/2 tsp kosher salt plus more
- 1 pint cherry tomatoes, halved
- Freshly ground black pepper
- 2 tbsp fresh lemon juice
- 1/2 cup of chopped fresh mint
- 2 scallions, thinly sliced
- 1 cup of quinoa, rinsed well
- 2/3 cup of chopped flat-leaf parsley
- 1/2 cup of extra-virgin olive oil
- 2 Persian cucumbers or 1 large English hothouse cucumber, cut it into 1/4" pieces1 garlic clove, minced

Instructions

1. In a medium saucepan, bring quinoa, 1/2 tsp of salt, and 1 1/4 cups of water to a boil over high heat. Now turn the heat down to medium-low, cover, and simmer for about 10 minutes, or until the quinoa is soft. Take it off the heat and cover it for 5 minutes. Use a fork to fluff.

2. In the meantime, mix garlic and lemon juice together in a small bowl. Whisk in the olive oil slowly. Add salt and pepper to taste to the dressing.

3   Now spread the quinoa out on a large baking sheet with a rim and let it cool. Move to a big bowl and mix in 1/4 cup of the dressing. DO AHEAD: Can be made up to 1 day ahead. Cover the rest of the dressing and the quinoa separately, and chill.

4   Put the quinoa in a bowl and add the cucumber, tomatoes, herbs, and scallions. Toss to coat. Salt and pepper can be added to taste. Drizzle remaining dressing over.

MEDITERRANEAN QUINOA SALAD

Prep Time: 15 Mins

Cook Time: 25 Mins

Total Time: 40 Mins

Serving: 8

Ingredients

- 1 tbsp balsamic vinegar
- ½ tsp kosher salt
- ½ cup of extra virgin olive oil
- 2 garlic cloves , pressed
- 1 ½ cups of dry quinoa
- ¼ cup of crumbled feta cheese
- 1 small jar roasted red bell peppers , that will be drained and chopped
- ½ tsp dried thyme , crushed between your fingers
- ¼ cup of Kalamata olives , pitted and roughly chopped

- 1 15 ounce can garbanzo beans , drained
- 3 cups of arugula
- kosher salt and freshly ground black pepper
- ½ tsp dry basil, minced

Instructions

1. First, cook the quinoa according to the directions on the package, adding 1/2 tsp of salt to the water. Cool off all the way.

2. Combine the olive oil, balsamic vinegar, garlic that has been pressed, basil, and thyme. Whisk until everything is well combined. Now add kosher salt and freshly ground black pepper, then set the dish aside.

3. Put the quinoa, arugula, garbanzo beans, roasted red peppers, Kalamata olives, and feta cheese in a large serving bowl.

4. Drizzle with the dressing, and then add basil on top. the way you like it. Serve food that's at room temperature.

ZESTY QUINOA SALAD

Prep Time: 5 Mins

Cook Time: 15 Mins

Total Time: 20 Mins

Serving: 12

Ingredients

- 1/4 cup of honey
- 2 cups of water
- 1/4 cup of olive oil

- 1 cup of quinoa rinsed
- 1/3 cup of white wine vinegar
- 1 cup of cucumber chopped (peel on)
- 1 1/2 cup of red and or yellow sweet bell peppers chopped
- salt and pepper to taste
- 1/2 cup of red onion finely chopped

Instructions

1. Rinse the quinoa for 1 to 2 minutes under cold water.
2. Add quinoa to the water in the bowl.
3. Now turn the heat down to medium and cook, covered, for 15 minutes or until all of the liquid has been absorbed. Use a fork to fluff.
4. While the quinoa is cooking, chop the red onion, bell peppers, and cucumber.
5. Put olive oil, vinegar, and honey in a small bowl. I put in about a tsp of salt and pepper, or more or less to taste, and mix well.
6. Once the quinoa is done, take it off the stove and pour it into a big bowl.
7. Mix together the peppers, onions, and oil and vinegar mixture.
8. Salt and pepper can be added to taste.

QUINOA AVOCADO SALAD

Prep Time: 15 Mins

Cook Time: 20 Mins

Total Time: 35 Mins

Serving: 6

Ingredients

Salad

- ¼ cup of chopped cilantro
- 1 cup of uncooked quinoa
- 2 large ripe avocados chopped
- 1 large cucumber diced
- 1 cup of grape tomatoes halved
- ¼ cup of red onion finely chopped

Dressing

- 1/4 cup of olive oil
- 1 tsp Dijon mustard
- 1 tbsp lime juice
- 1 tbsp red wine vinegar
- ½ tsp salt
- 1 garlic clove minced

Instructions

1   Put the quinoa in a medium sauce pan and turn the heat to medium. Toast the seeds for 5–7 minutes without oil or salt, until they start to pop and smell good. Now add 2 cups of water to the

quinoa, bring to a boil, and then turn the heat down to low. Cover the quinoa and let it simmer for 15 minutes. Take the pot off the heat and keep it covered for 10 more minutes. Salt and fluff the rice with a fork.

2   Mix the olive oil, red wine vinegar, lime juice, Dijon mustard, garlic, and salt together in a bowl with a whisk.

3   Once the quinoa is cool, put it in a bowl and add all the salad ingredients on top. Pour the dressing on top and gently mix it all together. Serve chilled or at room temperature.

QUINOA KALE SALAD

Prep Time: 15 Mins

Cook Time: 13 Mins

Total Time: 28 Mins

Serving: 6

Ingredients

- 1 + 1/4 cup of water
- 1/2 cup of crumbled feta cheese (skip if vegan)
- 2 cups of chopped kale
- 1/2 cup of of dry quinoa (tri color or regular white)
- 1 red bell pepper , chopped
- 1 can chickpeas that will be 15 ounce – drained and rinsed
- 1 cup of finely chopped broccoli florets
- 1/4 cup of sliced almonds
- 1/3-1/2 cup of finely chopped red onion

light lemon dressing

- 1 clove garlic
- 1/4 tsp black pepper
- 1.5lemons , juiced
- 1/8 tsp of dried dill or to taste (optional)
- 1/4 tsp of sea salt or extra, to taste
- 1 tsp white wine vinegar
- 3 TBSP of avocado oil or light olive oil

Instructions

1. First, use a mesh strainer or sieve to rinse and drain your quinoa. Put a small pot on medium heat and toast the quinoa, stirring often, to get rid of any extra water. This step is optional, but it really makes the quinoa taste nutty and fluffy. Next, add your water, turn your burner to high, and bring to a boil. When the water is boiling, turn the heat down to low, cover, and simmer for 12 to 13 minutes, or until the quinoa is fluffy and the liquid has been absorbed.

2. When your quinoa is done, fluff it with a fork and season it to taste with salt and pepper. Put in a medium bowl to cool down.

3. While the quinoa is cooking, clean and dry the chopped kale. Next, massage the kale with a drizzle of oil and a pinch of salt for a more tender, smooth texture and delicious taste.

4. Mix the kale with the chickpeas, bell pepper, broccoli, red onion, and sliced almonds. If you want some almonds in every bite, you can cut the almonds up small. Mix in quinoa.

5. Mix all the ingredients for the lemon dressing together and give it a taste. If you like the sour taste of lemon juice, which I do, You can eat it as is, or you can add a little more oil or sugar if you like.

Pour over the salad and mix well. Crumble some feta on top and enjoy!

6   You can eat it right away or let it chill. I like both versions! If you're making meals ahead, put them in the fridge and eat when you're ready. The salad will soak up the dressing, which will make the taste even stronger. Love it so!

LENTIL QUINOA SALAD

Prep Time: 25 Mins

Cook Time: 0 Mins

Total Time: 25 Mins

Serving: 4

Ingredients

- ½ cup of vegan feta , optional but recommended
- 2 cups of cooked lentils (I use Trader Joe's precooked refrigerated lentils for a fast version)
- 2 cups of fresh spinach , chopped
- 4 cups of cooked quinoa , use frozen for a fast version (about 1 ¼ cups of dry quinoa)
- ¾-1 tsp sea salt , taste and add more if needed
- 1 cup of roasted peppers , chopped (red, yellow or a mix, roast your own or use jarred for fast version)
- 1 tbsp balsamic vinegar
- 1 tbsp lemon juice , add more for extra tang if preferred
- ½ tsp ground ground black pepper

Instructions

1 Mix everything together in a bowl. Put in the fridge to chill. It tastes best cold, but you can also eat it warm.

2 If you cook quinoa or lentils the day before, add spinach to them while they are still warm. It will make the spinach wilt just a little.

3 If you're using jarred peppers that were packed in oil, give them a quick rinse or pat them dry with paper towels if you don't want any oil.

4 Serve alone or with other foods!

SOUTHWEST QUINOA SALAD

Prep Time: 15 Mins

Cook Time: 15 Mins

Total Time: 30 Mins

Serving: 5

Ingredients

For the salad:

- 1 red bell pepper, chopped
- 1 cup of canned corn, drained
- 2 tsp olive oil
- 4 green onions, sliced
- 2 cloves garlic, minced
- 1 3/4 cups of low sodium vegetable broth, or water
- 15 ounce of can black beans, rinsed and drained

- 2 tbsp minced fresh cilantro
- 1 cup of quinoa, well rinsed and drained

For The Lime Vinaigrette

- 3 tbsp fresh lime juice
- 1 tbsp honey
- 1/2 tsp cumin
- 2 tbsp olive oil
- 1 tsp chili powder salt and pepper, to taste

For Serving

- guacamole or avocado, if desired

Instructions

1 In a medium saucepan, heat the 2 tsp of olive oil over medium heat. Add the garlic and stir-fry it for about a minute, until it starts to smell good. Bring to a boil the quinoa, vegetable broth, or water. Now reduce the heat to low, cover, and simmer for 12 to 16 minutes, or until the liquid has been absorbed. Take off the heat.

2 Make the lime vinaigrette while the quinoa is cooking. Mix the ingredients for the dressing in a small bowl or jar. Now mix well with a whisk or shake in a jar with a lid.

3 Mix the corn, black beans, bell pepper, green onions, and cilantro into the cooked quinoa in a large bowl. Mix the dressing in with a gentle stir. Taste the food and change the seasonings as needed.

4 You can serve salad hot or cold. If you want, you can add guacamole or sliced avocado.

CAPRESE QUINOA SALAD

Prep Time: 10 Mins

Cook Time: 15 Mins

Total Time: 25 Mins

Serving: 4

Ingredients

- 10 leaves basil (cut chiffonade)
- 1 cup of quinoa
- 2 cups of chicken broth (low sodium)
- 1 cup of fresh mozzarella
- 1 cup of cherry tomatoes (sliced in half)
- 2 tbsp extra virgin olive oil (divided)
- Salt and pepper to taste
- 2 tbsp lemon juice

Instructions

1. In a medium pan, heat one tbsp of the olive oil over medium-high heat. Add half of the quinoa and toast it for 3 to 4 minutes, until it is lightly browned and smells good.

2. Add the chicken broth and heat until it starts to boil. Cover and turn down the heat. After 15 minutes, turn off the heat. Use a fork to fluff the quinoa, then set it aside.

3. Put the cooked quinoa, cherry tomatoes, mozzarella, basil, lemon juice, the last tbsp of olive oil, salt, and pepper in a medium bowl.

4. Mix the salad together by tossing it, and check the seasoning before you serve it.

CURRY QUINOA SALAD

Prep Time: 5 Mins

Cook Time: 20 Mins

Total Time: 25 Mins

Serving: 8

Ingredients

- ½ tsp sea salt
- ¾ cup of dried quinoa, rinsed
- ½ tsp mild yellow curry powder
- 1 ¼ cup of purified water

Dressing

- ¼ tsp turmeric
- ¾ tsp mild yellow curry powder
- ½ tsp sea salt
- ¼ cup of plain unsweetened Greek Yogurt (plain coconut yogurt works, too)
- 1 tsp apple cider vinegar
- ¼ tsp freshly ground black pepper
- ¼ cup of extra virgin olive oil

Veggies + Nuts

- ¼ cup of thinly sliced scallions, white and green parts

- 2 tbsp chopped cilantro
- ⅓ cup of slivered almonds (roasted cashews are a good substitute too)
- ½ cup of diced carrots (about 2 small or 1 large carrot)
- ⅓ cup of dried currants (or substitute raisins)

Instructions

1. First, make the quinoa. Put the quinoa in a fine-mesh strainer or colander and rinse it well for about 30 seconds, or until the water runs clear. Let the quinoa drain for a few seconds, then put the rinsed quinoa, salt, curry powder, and water in a medium saucepan.
2. Bring it to a boil, then cover and lower the heat to a simmer. Put a 12-minute timer on. Check it after 11 minutes. It's done when all the water has been soaked up. Don't let it go too long or it will stick to the pan.
3. When all the water has been absorbed, turn off the heat and fluff the rice with a fork. When cooked, 3/4 cup of dry quinoa will make 1.5 cups.
4. While the quinoa is cooking, mix all the ingredients for the dressing in the bottom of a large mixing bowl that is big enough to hold the whole salad. Then, prepare the vegetables. I find that the time it takes to make the dressing and cut up the vegetables is about right for letting the quinoa cook.
5. Once the quinoa is done cooking, add it to the dressing while it is still warm. Now add rest of the ingredients and mix everything together.
6. Let it cool in the refrigerator for at least 30 to 60 minutes.

MACARONI SALAD

HAWAIIAN MACARONI
SALAD

Prep Time: 10 Minutes

Cook Time: 15 Minutes

Additional Time: 30 Minutes

Total Times: 55 Minutes

Serving: 10-12

Ingredients

- 2 cups of milk
- 2 large celery stalks, diced small
- 1 tsp slat
- 4-5 green onions, diced small
- 1 tsp pepper
- 2 Tbsp brown sugar
- 1/4 cup of apple cider vinegar
- 1 big carrot, peeled and grated
- 1 pound elbow macaroni
- 2 cups of mayonnaise

Instructions

1   In a medium bowl, whisk together milk, mayonnaise, brown sugar, salt, and pepper until smooth. This will be the dressing. Refrigerate until needed.

2   Bring a lot of salted water to a rolling boil in a large pot. Add the macaroni and cook for about 10 to 12 minutes, until it is very soft but not mushy.

3   Drain the pasta and put it back in the pot. Pour vinegar over the pasta right away and toss it well. Let it cool for 10 minutes while it's covered.

4   Add half of dressing to the cooked pasta and stir well to coat the macaroni all over. Cover again for 20 minutes so that the pasta can soak up the dressing.

5   Mix the pasta well with the rest of the dressing, the green onions, celery, and grated carrot. Taste the food and add salt and pepper as needed.

6   Cover and chill for at least 2 hours in the fridge before serving. Mix the food gently before serving.

CLASSIC MACARONI SALAD

Prep Time: 10 Minutes

Cook Time: 20 Minutes

Total Times: 30 Minutes

Serving: 6

Ingredients

Salad Ingredients

- 1/2 cup of red onion, diced
- 1/2 cup of celery, diced
- 2 large hard-boiled eggs
- 2 cups of elbow macaroni, uncooked
- 1 cup of red bell peppers, diced
- 1 Tbsp chopped parsley, optional for garnish

Dressing Ingredients

- 3 tsp yellow mustard
- 1/2 cup of mayonnaise
- 1 tsp ground black pepper
- 3 tbsp apple cider vinegar
- 1 tsp salt, adjust to taste
- 3 tbsp sweet relish

Instructions

1 Follow the directions on the box for cooking elbow macaroni in salted water. Now drain the pasta and run it under cold water to clean it. Then set it aside.

2 In a separate bowl, whisk together all the ingredients for the dressing until the mixture is smooth and creamy.

3 Put the mac and cheese in a big bowl. Mix in the diced bell peppers, red onion, celery, and eggs.

4 Pour the dressing into the bowl and stir to mix. If you want, garnish with parsley and serve right away, or cover and put in the fridge until you're ready to eat.

CAJUN MACARONI SALAD

Prep Time: 20 Minutes

Cook Time: 10 Minutes

Total Times: 30 Minutes

Serving: 10

Ingredients

- 2 tsp Cajun seasoning preferably no salt blend
- Kosher salt and freshly, cracked black pepper
- 1 tsp hot sauce
- 3 tbsp red wine vinegar
- ½ sweet onion, minced like Vidalia
- 1 tsp freshly, cracked black pepper
- 4 ribs celery, small dice
- 1 tsp smoked paprika
- 3 tbsp Creole mustard
- ½ lemon, juiced
- 1 tbsp olive oil
- 1 pound elbow macaroni
- 1½ cups of good quality mayonnaise and 2 hard boiled eggs, small dice
- Optional: ½ tsp cayenne pepper, Chopped parsley, sliced boiled egg, for garnish.

Instructions

1 Bring some water to a boil and add a lot of salt to it. Follow the directions on the box to cook macaroni. Drain the water, rinse with cold water, repeat, and put the water in a big bowl. Mix with olive oil and set aside.

2 In the meantime, mix the rest of the ingredients together in another bowl. Use a whisk to mix together everything else except for the celery, onion, and egg. Start with 2 tsp of salt and 2 tbsp of water, and add more water as needed, up to 14 cup of. Stir in the celery, onion, and egg when everything is mixed. The sauce shouldn't be too thick, but it shouldn't be too thin either.

3 Taste the sauce to see if it needs more salt, pepper, or hot sauce. Mix into the elbows that have already been cooked. Serve right

away with fresh parsley and/or slices of hardboiled egg, or put it in the fridge until you're ready to eat. If you need to, add a little water to loosen it up and make it shiny again.

CHICKEN MACARONI SALAD

Prep Time: 10 Minutes

Cook Time: 10 Minutes

Total Times: 20 Minutes

Serving: 10

Ingredients

- 1 medium red bell pepper, finely diced
- 1/2 tsp seasoned salt
- 2 celery ribs, finely diced
- 2 tsp dijon mustard
- 1/2 tbsp apple cider vinegar
- 2 (12.5-ounce) cans chunk chicken breast, drained
- 2 hard-boiled eggs, chopped
- 1 1/2 cups of mayonnaise
- 1/2 medium red onion, finely diced
- 1/3 cup of sweet relish
- 3 1/2 cups of uncooked macaroni pasta

Instructions

1   Follow the directions on the package to cook macaroni until it is al dente. Drain.

2   Mix mayonnaise, Dijon mustard, relish, and vinegar together in a large bowl.

3   Add the pasta, chicken, hard-boiled egg, red onion, red bell pepper, seasoned salt, and celery. Stir in order to mix.

4   Check the seasoning, and if it needs salt or pepper, add it.

5   Finally, refrigerate it for at least 2 hours before serving.

MACARONI SALAD WITH PROSCIUTTO

Prep Time: 10 Minutes

Cook Time: 13 Minutes

Total Times: 23 Minutes

Serving: 8

Ingredients

- 1 tbsp pickle juice
- 3 ounce prosciutto
- 1 cup of mayonnaise
- 1/4 tsp pepper
- 1 tbsp white vinegar
- 1/4 cup of milk
- 1/2 cup of olives, chopped
- 2 roasted red peppers, chopped
- 12 ounce dry elbow macaroni
- 6 medium pickles, chopped

- 4 green onions, chopped
- 1/4 tsp salt

Instructions

1. Follow the directions on the box to cook macaroni.
2. In a small bowl, mix the mayonnaise, vinegar, salt, and pepper together with a whisk. Add some pickle juice, as much as you want, along with the milk, and mix well. If you need to, add more milk. The dressing should be thin enough to pour.
3. You shouldn't need to add any oil to the pan as you cook the prosciutto until it gets crispy.
4. Mix the cooked macaroni, crispy prosciutto, olives, pickles, roasted red peppers, green onions, and dressing together in a large bowl.
5. Use cold food.

MEXICAN MACARONI SALAD

Prep Time: 20 Minutes

Cook Time: 10 Minutes

Total Times: 30 Minutes

Serving: 8

Ingredients

- 1/2 cup of of Cotija cheese, broken up
- 3 large Roma tomatoes, peeled and cut into small pieces (1 1/2 cups)
- 1/3 cup of of chopped, washed red onion or 2/3 cup of of chopped, washed green onion (or use a blend of both)

- 10 ounce dry elbow macaroni
- 2 husked ears of fresh yellow corn
- Salt and black pepper that has just been ground
- 1 can of black beans, well rinsed and drained
- 1 large avocado (semi-firm but ripe), diced

Dressing

- 1/2 tsp ground cumin
- 1 tsp ancho chili powder
- 2 1/2 Tbsp fresh lime juice
- 1/4 cup of finely minced fresh cilantro (about small 1 bunch, leaf portion)
- 1/2 cup of mayonnaise (full fat)
- 1/2 cup of plain Greek yogurt (fat free)
- 1 clove garlic, minced

Instructions

1. Bring a grill up to about 450 degrees F over medium-high heat. Once the grill is hot, add the corn and turn it every 2–3 minutes until all sides are charred, which will take about 8– 9 minutes. Set aside and let cool before cutting the kernels off the cobs.
2. Meantime, cook the pasta in lightly salted water (about 1/2 tsp) until it is al dente, following the directions on the package. Drain and rinse, then let cool and drain again.
3. For the dressing, mix mayonnaise, Greek yogurt, lime juice, cilantro, garlic, chili powder, cumin, and salt and pepper to taste (about 3/4 tsp of salt and 1/4 tsp of pepper) in a mixing bowl. Chill until ready to assemble macaroni salad.
4. Set aside some of the ingredients you'll be mixing in (tomatoes, corn, avocado, and onion, if you want the salad to have some color on top). Mix the drained macaroni, corn kernels, tomatoes,

black beans, avocado, Cotija cheese, onion, and cilantro dressing mixture together in a salad bowl. Sprinkle set aside ingredients over top.

5   Serve right away or let it chill for up to 2 hours (thin with a little water if desired, it thickens as it rests since the noodles absorb the liquid).

BACON AND AVOCADO MACARONI SALAD

Prep Time: 10 Minutes

Cook Time: 10 Minutes

Total Times: 20 Minutes

Serving: 4

Ingredients

- Kosher salt and freshly ground black pepper
- 5 slices bacon, diced
- 2 avocados, halved, seeded, peeled and diced
- 12 ounces elbows pasta
- 2 tsp fresh thyme leaves, for garnish

For The Lemon Thyme Dressing

- ⅓ cup of olive oil
- ¼ cup of freshly squeezed lemon juice
- 1 tbsp sugar
- 1 ½ tbsp lemon zest
- ¾ cup of mayonnaise

- Kosher salt and freshly ground black pepper
- 1 tsp fresh thyme leaves

Instructions

1   To make the dressing, put mayonnaise, lemon juice, lemon zest, sugar, and thyme in the bowl of a food processor. Add salt and pepper to taste. While the motor is on, slowly pour in the olive oil until the mixture is smooth. Set aside.

2   Now, cook pasta according to the directions on the package in a large pot of salted water that is boiling. Then, drain well.

3   Put a large pan over medium-high heat to heat up. Add the bacon and cook for about 6 to 8 minutes, until it is brown and crispy. Move to a plate lined with a paper towel.

4   Mix the pasta, bacon, avocado, lemon-thyme dressing, salt and pepper in a large bowl.

5   Serve right away with thyme on top.

AMISH MACARONI SALAD

Prep Time: 15 Minutes

Cook Time: 10 Minutes

Total Times: 25 Minutes

Serving: 12

Ingredients

- ¾ tsp celery seed
- 3 large hard boiled eggs, chopped
- ¼ tsp salt
- 2 cups of creamy salad dressing
- ¾ cup of white sugar
- 2 cups of uncooked elbow macaroni
- 3 ¼ tsp apple cider vinegar
- 3 stalks celery, chopped
- 3 tbsp prepared yellow mustard
- 3 tbsp sweet pickle relish
- 1 cup of diced red bell pepper
- 1 cup of diced onion

Instructions

1   Bring a pot of water with a little salt to a boil.

2   Add the elbow macaroni to a pot of boiling water and cook until it is al dente, which usually takes about 8 minutes. Drain, then set it aside to cool down. (do not rinse!)

3   Mix the macaroni, eggs, onion, celery, and red bell pepper in a large bowl.

4   Now mix together salad dressing, pickle relish, mustard, white sugar, vinegar, salt, and celery seed in a small bowl using a whisk. Then pour the dressing over salad and toss to coat.

5   Before serving, cover and put in the fridge for at least an hour.

DEVILED EGG MACARONI SALAD

Prep Time: 20 Minutes

Cook Time: 10 Minutes

Total Times: 25 Minutes

Serving: 30

Ingredients

- ½ tsp smoked paprika
- 2 ribs celery, chopped
- ½ cup of black olives, sliced
- 2 tbsp Dijon mustard
- ¼ tsp salt
- ¼ tsp black pepper
- 12 ounces elbow macaroni, uncooked
- 3 medium dill pickles, chopped
- ½ medium red onion, chopped
- 8 large eggs, hard boiled
- 1 tbsp chives, chopped
- 1 cup of mayonnaise

Instructions

1. Get the pasta ready. Use the box as a guide and follow the cooking instructions on the box. After you strain, give it a good rinse with cold water.

2. Get the eggs ready. Peel and cut the eggs in half. Take the yolks out and put them in a bowl. Chopped up the egg whites.

3. Get ready the sauce. Use a fork to mash the yolks until they are smooth. Salt and pepper them, then add the mustard and mayonnaise. Mix everything together well.

4. Put the salad together. Put the macaroni in a big bowl to mix. Mix in the dressing, the egg whites, the rest of the ingredients, and the paprika. Mix everything together until the dressing covers it all.

5. Finish it off and serve. Sprinkle smoke paprika and chives on the salad, and then eat it.

TUNA AVOCADO MACARONI SALAD

Prep Time: 20 Minutes

Total Times: 20 Minutes

Serving: 4

Ingredients

- 1 green red bell pepper
- diced salt and pepper to taste
- 2 Tbsp cider vinegar
- 1 Tbsp dijon mustard
- 2 avocados diced

- 1/2 cup of shredded carrots
- 8 ounces elbow macaroni
- 5 ounce white albacore tuna drained
- 1 cup of mayonnaise
- 1 red bell pepper diced
- 1 small red onion diced
- 1 Tbsp sugar

Instructions

1. Put elbow macaroni in a large pot and bring it to a boil. Cook until al dente, then run cold water through a colander to clean.
2. Put pasta, tuna, carrots, red onion, bell peppers, and avocado in a large bowl. In a small bowl, mix together the dijon mustard, cider vinegar, sugar, and mayonnaise. Pour over the pasta and toss to coat. Add chopped chives and freshly cracked salt and pepper if you want. Serve it right away or put it in the fridge, but add the avocado right before you serve it.

FILIPINO CHICKEN MACARONI SALAD

Prep Time: 10 Minutes

Cook Time: 35 Minutes

Total Times: 45 Minutes

Serving: 8

Ingredients

- 1/4 cup of sweet relish
- 1 1/2 cups of Lady's Choice Mayonnaise
- 1 lb elbow macaroni and 1 cup of carrot chopped
- 1/4 tsp ground black pepper
- 1 pound boneless chicken breast
- 1 piece green bell pepper chopped
- 1 1/2 cups of shredded cheddar cheese
- 3 tsp salt this will be used when boiling chicken and macaroni
- Water for boiling and 1 cup of raisins
- 1 bottle pimiento 6.5 ounce chopped
- 1/2 tsp garlic powder

Instructions

1   Get the chicken ready. Start boiling the chicken by pouring 1 quart of water into a pot on the stove and putting it on the burner. Put on the heat and let it boil. Put the chicken breasts in the pot and add 1 tsp of salt. Cover and boil for 22 minutes over medium heat. Take the chicken out of the pan. Let it get cooler. Shred by hand into small pieces and set them aside.

2   Follow the directions on the box to make the mac and cheese. Now bring 3 quarts of water to a boil. Add 1 tsp salt. Put the mac and cheese in the pot. Stir. Cover the pot and continue to boil the macaroni over medium heat for 9 minutes, or until it is al dente. Make sure to stir the mac and cheese every 3 minutes so it doesn't stick together. Get rid of the water. Set macaroni aside.

3   Set up the macaroni in a big bowl. Add shredded chicken. Toss.

4   Put in pineapple, pimento, green bell pepper, raisins, carrot, sweet relish, and cheese. Toss until everything is mixed together.

5   Add lady's Choice Mayonnaise and garlic powder. Mix everything together gently.

6   Finally add salt and ground black pepper to taste. Serve! Enjoy it with your family.

PUERTO RICAN SHRIMP MACARONI SALAD

Prep Time: 10 Minutes

Cook Time: 15 Minutes

Rest Times: 30 Minutes

Total Times: 55 Minutes

Serving: 8

Ingredients

Salad

- 5 hard boiled eggs peeled and chopped
- Tajin seasoning to garnish
- ½ red bell pepper chopped
- 8 ounce elbow macaroni cooked and drained
- 2 tbsp of red onion finely chopped
- 1 carrot peeled and finely chopped
- 1 celery stalk minced
- 1 ½ cups of cooked shrimp peeled and deveined

Sauce

- ½-1 tsp of mustard
- ¼ cup of mayonnaise
- ¼-1/2 tsp of lemon juice or to taste
- 1 tsp of granulated white sugar
- ¼ tsp of adobo seasoning or salt

Instructions

- First, put all the salad ingredients into a large bowl.
- Whisk the sauce ingredients together in a medium bowl, and taste to see if they need to be changed.
- Pour the sauce mixture over the salad and fold it together gently.
- Finallly, cover the salad and refrigerate it for at least 30 minutes before serving.

ITALIAN MACARONI SALAD

Prep Time: 15 Minutes

Cook Time: 5 Minutes

Total Times: 20 Minutes

Serving: 8

Ingredients

- 1 and 1/2 tsp Italian seasoning
- 1 cup of frozen peas, thawed
- 3/4 cup of zesty Italian salad dressing
- 1/4 cup of apple cider vinegar
- 1 red bell pepper, remove seeds and diced
- 1 pound elbow macaroni noodles
- 1/3 cup of red onion, diced
- 4 ribs of celery, diced
- 3/4 cup of mayonnaise
- 4 ounces sharp provolone cheese, cubed
- 4 ounce genoa salami, sliced salt and pepper, to taste

Instructions

1. Bring a lot of salted water to a boil in a large pot. Now, add macaroni and cook for about 5 minutes, or until it is al dente.
2. After draining the pasta, rinse it in cold water until it is cool.
3. While the water is heating up, cut up your meat, cheese, and vegetables.
4. Put the pasta in a big bowl and put it aside.

5   Mix the Italian dressing, mayonnaise, vinegar, Italian seasoning, salt, and pepper well in a medium-sized mixing bowl until everything is smooth and combined.

6   Mix well to coat the pasta with the dressing.

7   Add the vegetables, cheese, and salami to the bowl of pasta. Mix well, and then add salt and pepper to taste. Serve right away or chill until you need it.

VEGAN AMACRONI SALAD

Prep Time: 30 Minutes

Total Times: 30 Minutes

Serving: 8

Ingredients

- 1/8 tsp pepper
- 1 celery rib, chopped
- 1 small carrot, chopped
- 1/4 tsp salt
- Dash paprika
- 1/4 cup of chopped onion
- 3/4 tsp ground mustard
- 1 cup of vegan mayonnaise
- 2 tbsp sweet pickle relish
- 2 cups of uncooked elbow macaroni

Instructions

1   Follow the directions on the box to cook the macaroni, then drain and rinse with cold water. Cool all the way.

2   In a small mixing bowl, combine and mix together mayonnaise, pickle relish, mustard, salt, and pepper to make the dressing. Mix the macaroni, celery, carrot, and onion together in a large bowl. Add the sauce and gently toss to coat.

3   Refrigerate until serving. Sprinkle paprika on top.

MIDDLE EASTERN INSPIRED MACARONI SALAD

Prep Time: 25 Minutes

Total Times: 25 Minutes

Serving: 8

Ingredients

- 2 tsp sugar
- 3/4 tsp ground mustard
- 1 can (16 ounces) garbanzo beans or chickpeas, rinsed and drained
- 1/8 tsp pepper
- 1 cup of mayonnaise
- 1/4 cup of chopped onion
- 1 to 2 tsp za'atar seasoning
- 1/2 pound ground lamb
- 1/4 tsp salt
- 2 cups of uncooked elbow macaroni
- Optional toppings: plain yogurt and lemon zest

Instructions

1 Follow the directions on the box to cook the macaroni, then drain and rinse with cold water. Cool all the way. In the meantime, cook the lamb in a small pan over medium heat until it's no longer pink, about 6-7 minutes, breaking it up as you go. Drain. Set aside to cool all the way down.

2 For dressing, place the mayonnaise, sugar, mustard, salt, and pepper in a small mixing bowl then stir them together. Mix the chickpeas, onion, za'atar seasoning, macaroni, and lamb in a large bowl. Now add the dressing and toss gently to coat.

3 Refrigerate until serving. If you want, you can add yogurt and lemon zest on top.

MACARONI COLESLAW

Prep Time: 25 Minutes

Total Times: 25 Minutes

Serving: 16

Ingredients

- 1 medium green pepper, finely chopped
- 1 package (14 ounces) coleslaw mix
- 1 package (7 ounces) of ring macaroni or ditalini
- 2 celery ribs, chopped
- 1 can (8 ounces) of whole water chestnuts, drained and finely chopped
- 2 medium onions, finely chopped
- 1 medium cucumber, finely chopped

Dressing

- 1/2 tsp salt
- 1/4 cup of cider vinegar
- 1/4 tsp pepper
- 1/3 cup of sugar
- 1-1/2 cups of Miracle Whip Light

Instructions

1 Cook the macaroni following the instructions on the package. Once cooked, drain the water and rinse the macaroni with cold water. Transfer the macaroni to a large bowl. Add the coleslaw mix, onions, celery, cucumber, green pepper, and water chestnuts.

2 In a small mix bowl, combine and whisk the dressing ingredients. Pour over salad; toss to coat. Finally, cover and refrigerate for at least 1 hour.

BARBECUE MACARONI
SALAD

Prep Time: 20 Minutes

Total Times: 20 Minutes

Serving: 5

Ingredients

- 2 hard-boiled large eggs, chopped
- 2 tsp sugar

- 1 to 3 tbsp barbecue sauce
- 2 cups of uncooked elbow macaroni
- 1/8 tsp pepper
- 1/4 tsp salt
- 3/4 tsp ground mustard
- 1 tbsp ranch salad dressing mix
- 2 tbsp sweet pickle relish
- 1 cup of mayonnaise

Instructions

1. Follow the directions on the box to cook the macaroni, then drain and rinse with cold water. Cool all the way.
2. For the dressing, mix mayonnaise, barbecue sauce, ranch dressing mix, sugar, mustard, salt, and pepper together in a small bowl.
3. Mix the eggs, relish, and macaroni in a big bowl. Add dressing and toss gently to coat.
4. Refrigerate until serving.
5. If you want, drizzle with more barbecue sauce.

GRECIAN INSPIRED MACARONI SALAD

Prep Time: 25 Minutes

Total Times: 25 Minutes

Serving: 9

Ingredients

- 1/2 cup of sliced red onion
- 3/4 tsp ground mustard
- 1/2 cup of cherry tomatoes, halved
- 1/8 tsp pepper
- 2 tsp sugar
- 1/2 cup of crumbled feta cheese
- 1/4 cup of Greek olives, chopped
- 2 cups of uncooked elbow macaroni
- 2 tsp grated lemon zest
- 1 cup of mayonnaise
- 1/2 cup of chopped peeled cucumber
- 1/4 tsp salt
- 2 tsp dried oregano

Instructions

1. Follow the directions on the box to cook the macaroni, then drain and rinse with cold water. Cool all the way.
2. In a small bowl, combine and mix together the mayonnaise, sugar, oregano, lemon zest, mustard, salt, and pepper to make the dressing.
3. Mix the feta, cucumber, onion, tomatoes, olives, and macaroni in a large bowl. Now add dressing and toss gently to coat.
4. Refrigerate until serving.

CUBANO MACARONI SALAD

Prep Time: 25 Minutes

Total Times: 25 Minutes

Serving: 10

Ingredients

- 1/2 cup of chopped sweet pickles
- 1 cup of cubed fully cooked ham
- 1 cup of cubed cooked pork
- 1/2 cup of chopped onion
- 1 cup of mayonnaise
- 2 tsp sugar
- 3/4 tsp ground mustard
- 2 cups of uncooked elbow macaroni
- 1/8 tsp pepper
- 1/4 tsp salt
- 1 cup of shredded Swiss cheese

Instructions

1. Follow the directions on the box to cook the macaroni, then drain and rinse with cold water. Cool all the way.
2. For the dressing, put mayonnaise, sugar, mustard, salt, and pepper in a small mixing bowl and stir them together.
3. Mix the cheese, pork, ham, pickles, onion, and macaroni together in a large bowl. Add dressing and toss gently to coat.
4. Refrigerate until serving.